The Christmas Killings

40 Hours to Justice

STEPHEN C. GRISMER   JUDITH M. MONSEUR
&
DENNIS A. MURPHY

PUBLISHED BY
DAYTON POLICE HISTORY FOUNDATION, INC.

JUDITH M. MONSEUR
DENNIS A. MURPHY
STEPHEN C. GRISMER

This book was produced with the generous
assistance of the Dayton law firm
DOLL, JANSEN & FORD

Copyright © December 2017 by Stephen C. Grismer

The contents of this book are the authors' own research
and interpretation of this aspect of history.

Contributing editors: BRIAN FORSCHNER, SUSAN JANSEN,
DEBORAH MILLER, M. RUTH MYERS & RICK NAGEL

Interview filming and images by
AMY M. SIMPSON
and
Cover design by
AUSTIN KIRKPATRICK
Copyright © December 2017 by
Dayton Police History Foundation, Inc.

All rights reserved. The text of this publication, or any part thereof,
may not be reproduced in any manner whatsoever without
written permission from the authors / publisher.

Library of Congress Control Number: 2017918614

ISBN-10: 0-9895302-3-X
ISBN-13: 978-0-9895302-3-1

Produced in the United States of America
10 9 8 7 6 5 4 3 2 1

Published by
DPH FOUNDATION, INC.
P.O. Box 293157
DAYTON, OH 45429-9157
www.DaytonPoliceHistory.org

DEDICATION

This book is dedicated to all law enforcement officers, particularly members of the Dayton Police Department.

May they all stay safe in their duties as they serve and protect our communities.

IN MEMORY OF
TOMMY XARHOULACOS
MARCH 24, 1935 TO MARCH 12, 2018

Owner "Tommy X" *(right)* seated with friends at *The Embassy*

REMEMBERING
THE MORAINE EMBASSY
JANUARY 1, 1969 TO JUNE 16, 2013

ACKNOWLEDGEMENTS

This book is the product of three writers but there are many individuals, and a few organizations, deserving of recognition and our sincerest thanks. Their respective contributions are identified with their names. *Our gratitude goes to:*

The law firm of **Doll, Jansen & Ford** for the use of its office facilities and material support. Over the past five years, countless hours were spent brainstorming, reviewing filmed interviews, writing and editing in the conference rooms of Suite 1100.

The four Dayton officers interviewed: retired Dayton Homicide Sergeant **Larry Grossnickle** and retired Dayton Homicide Detectives **Wade Lawson, Thomas Lawson** and **A. Doyle Burke**. After years away from the murder cases, they willingly assembled and agreed to hours-long filmed interviews, providing their first-hand account of the case.

The co-owners of The Moraine Embassy – **Tom Xarhoulacos** and **Jim Xarhoulacos** and late brother **Bill Xarhoulacos** – for the use of their establishment for our interviews. The caricatures of the "X" brothers on the opening page (i) appear behind the detectives (left to right: Jimmy X, Bill X, Tommy X).

Tommy's better half, retired Dayton Fugitive Detective **Donna Pack**, introduced our concept so as to secure the use of the brothers' place. Arrangements to close the bar for filming were made by the kind and ever-salty barkeep, **Janet Bell**.

Dayton Cold Case Detective **Patricia Tackett** was especially accommodating in providing access to police case files as was Montgomery County Chief Criminal Prosecutor **Leon Daidone** who contributed supporting material.

Retired Dayton Police Lieutenant **John Huber** pleased us immensely by unexpectedly offering an audio tape of the 1992 police dispatch transmissions. *It is quoted verbatim in this story.* He diagrammed the arrest sequence which was used as the basis for four illustrated maps found in Chapter 4. He also provided a few personal pictures upon request as did retired Dayton Police Sergeant **Moises Perez**.

Austin Kirkpatrick offered his expertise with digital conversion of the dispatch tape and imagery enhancement, but his greatest contribution was in the graphic design of the front and back sides of the book cover. It certainly captures the essence of the story and immediate attention.

Retired Montgomery County Chief Criminal Prosecutor **James Levinson**, the successful trial attorney for the case against the killers, kindly reviewed an early completed version of the manuscript.

Others who thoughtfully critiqued the script were local attorney, **Susan Jansen**, Esq., Dayton Municipal Court judges, the Honorable **Daniel Gehres** and the Honorable **Christopher Roberts**, retired Montgomery County Victim/Witness Advocate, **Lisa Budenz** (Lisa Edwards in 1992), and retired Ohio State Highway Patrol Sergeant **David Durr**.

Other individuals had a hand in the production of this book. The very necessary transcribing of the interviews and dispatch transmissions were precisely done by **Shilo Draime** and **Dolores Monseur**.

Not fully satisfied that the complexity of the story was readily clear, we asked several friends for an assessment of the last draft and some final edits: **Susan Jansen**, again, as well as by novelist **M. Ruth Myers**, author **Brian Forschner**, information technology business CFO **Rick Nagel**, and retired educator **Deborah Miller**. Proof reading was attentively done by local attorney **Matt Crawford** and business manager **Kathy Nagel**.

Many other individuals and organizations graciously provided photographs and images. Some are credited beneath their photographs, but most are credited on page 119. **Chris Tung**, a film production specialist, has given his time to our early work and remains an available resource.

The editor of Dayton History Books Online and local book author, **Curt Dalton**, was generous with his time in setting in motion the formatting of this book.

There is no doubt that this book would not have been possible had it not been for former Dayton Police Officer **Amy Simpson**, a talented artist and photographer. She conducted the dual-camera filming of the interviews, the basis of this book. She has an eye for lighting and uncommon angles. The photo images captured of the principals are her vision and a wonderful gift to us to share in words and, hopefully someday, with a documentary production.

We should note that the private non-profit organization, **Dayton Police History Foundation, Inc.**, motivates all research that is conducted on local law enforcement and garners warm support.

Thank you.

DAYTON, OHIO CIRCA 1992

Aerial view of Downtown Dayton looking west toward the Great Miami River

THE ROLE OF THE HOMICIDE DETECTIVE

"The role of the homicide detective it is to tell the story of what happened, who it happened to and who did it. You analyze the minute details, the nuances of the incident, the forensic evidence. You try to use reasonable objectiveness and common sense to solve the homicide.

"If the death turns out to be criminal, then you present the facts and circumstance for the jury in a way that they become a witness to the tragic events when they have no first-hand knowledge of the murder."

—*Detective Dennis Murphy*
Dayton Homicide Squad
2009-2016

THE DOWNTOWN DAYTON CHRISTMAS PARADE

Circa 1990 - West Second Street en route to North Main Street

DAYTON'S COURTHOUSE SQUARE

1992 DOWNTOWN DAYTON ACTIVITY
at the bus stop on West Third Street
alongside the Old Court House,
across from the Arcade Center

THE OLD COURT HOUSE
Constructed in 1847, it is Dayton's landmark at the center of town.

Corner of North Main at West Third Streets

Table of Contents

"Attention All Crews!"

"What do you mean, 'He's not here?'"

"Frank-Mary-Boston 1-8-6"

"That car is moving. The Shadow's moving!"

"I wanted them to be Bonnie and Clyde."

The Fleeing Killer

Piecing Together the Evidence

"They partied in his house for several days."
Revelation for the Homicide Squad

"Hey, put some drama in your life."
Interrogations Part 1

"Merry Christmas bitch."
Interrogations Part 2

"BOOM! She just pulls out a gun and shoots him."
Interrogations Part 3

"It just never ended."
Interrogations Part 4

Revelation and Recovery

"Laura Taylor told me."

"I mean, these were friends."
Discovery by the Homicide Squad

Reflections: The Viciousness of the Crimes

Prosecution and Sentencing

Justice and Closure

IN MEMORIAM

The Network

"The Downtown Posse" - Direct traveling routes to three gang hangouts

This true-life crime drama opens Christmas week. The very first crime to come to the attention of four Dayton homicide detectives occurs the evening of **December 24, 1992**. The ensuing incidents that they encounter span **40 consecutive hours** until resolved, thus touching three days. The full story unfolds through the four-day holiday weekend, and then presses onward into the weeks and months that follow.

THE HOLIDAY DAYS

Christmas Eve, **Thursday**
Christmas Day, **Friday**
Day After Christmas, **Saturday**
Christmas Sunday

The reader will quickly come to know the homicide detectives, but within the brief 40-hour window during which they investigate the killers, three haunts and 10 individuals emerge as collateral figures to the story. What follows for the reader is the network reference guide.

THE NETWORK: "THE DOWNTOWN POSSE"

THE THREE "POSSE" HANGOUTS

Bill McIntyre's Apartment
159 Yuma Place

Joe Wilkerson's House
3321 Prescott Avenue

Sandra Pinson's House
729 Kumler Avenue

The Two Core Couples

Marvallous Keene & Laura Taylor

Demarcus Smith & Heather Mathews

Two Companion Couples

Nick Woodson & Melissa Gomez
Woodson: Sandra Pinson's nephew

Marvin Washington & Wendy Cottrill

Three Close Connections

Deon Pinson
Sandra Pinson's son
Nick Woodson's cousin

Jeffrey Wright
Heather Mathew's ex-boyfriend

Richmond Maddox
Laura Taylor's ex-boyfriend

Mobility: The Three Cars

Red 1974 Buick Electra

Blue 1989 Pontiac Grand Am

Black 1988 Dodge Shadow

INTRODUCTION

The Protagonists – Dayton Homicide Detectives

Although it is not unusual for a book to be penned by a pair of writers, it is out of the ordinary for one to be a collaboration by three authors. This is the case with *The Christmas Killings: 40 Hours to Justice*. How this book came about is also out of the ordinary.

Beginning in 2010, Dennis, Judith and I spent well over a year filming 30 interviews for a prospective documentary production recounting the unique history of Dayton, Ohio law enforcement – after all, the notorious fugitive, John Dillinger, was taken down by Dayton detectives in 1933. Then, most suddenly, our efforts were suspended because of an inspirational moment. Judith and I are quick to point our fingers at our younger associate: **Dennis Murphy**.

In the spring of 2012, Dennis was a 12-year veteran of the Dayton Police Department and a member of the Dayton homicide squad. He realized that the 20th anniversary of, arguably, Dayton's most shocking murder spree was approaching – the 1992 "Christmas Killings." He believed it was a story that needed to be captured in a separate documentary and there was no better way than to tap into the thoughts and feelings of the four men who were called out to investigate the homicides over a weekend when other people were engaged in joyous holiday festivities.

This investigation was even more compelling to Dennis because the detectives are widely recognized as being among Dayton's most renowned and respected criminal investigators – **Sgt. Larry Grossnickle, Det. Wade Lawson**, his brother, **Det. Tom Lawson**, and **Det. Doyle Burke**. This story is told from their perspective – both in the way events unfolded in 1992 and in the way these distinguished officers recall the events.

Traditionally, Dayton detectives have a daily eight-hour tour of duty. They report by 8 a.m. for roll call and to view prisoners arrested overnight on the "show up" stage. It is not unusual for police officers, in general, to find their tours extended beyond normal work hours.

Homicide detectives, however, are subject to being called in at all times of the day, evening and night to respond to fresh crime scenes. This is a police "call out" – an after-hour work assignment.

Homicide detectives are called out to investigate not only death scenes, but also shootings, stabbings, beatings or any serious assault that could lead to death. The members of the Dayton homicide squad, being a unit of only four detectives under the direction of a detective sergeant, often work throughout the day and night to gather clues that lead them to solve murders.

As a homicide detective, Dennis Murphy accepts – as do all homicide investigators – the undeniable hardships brought on by their chosen assignment.

"In my experience, 'working homicide' is a marathon. It's truly a sacrifice. While extremely demanding in your professional life, what you don't realize is you give up your personal life as well. The daily grind consists of long hours in court, working after hours chasing leads, locating witnesses, searching for evidence, and losing sleep because you get called out to violent crime scenes anytime, day or night. You reschedule vacations because of court trials or you get a fresh tip on a case that demands immediate attention. There are times you're a stranger in your own home. Because you dedicate your life to solving murders, you come home days later to learn about the events your family experienced they forget you missed. There are no weekends or holidays – every day is Monday. However, we readily accept this undertaking for the greater good; to bring about justice and to make our community a safer place."

And so it was in 1992.

Dennis was clear that he wanted this story told from the point of view of the investigators – the protagonists. And, he wanted to film the four homicide detectives, all retired, in a familiar setting where police officers typically share lively memories and ponder sobering experiences. "The Embassy," as readers will discover, was the natural choice.

What started as an Embassy interview for a documentary was reimagined by Judith, Dennis and me as a filmed interview depicted in a book ... this book. The account is expressed in present tense – whether it is 1992 or 2012 – and delivered as if by screen narration.

As the three of us examined the case file, time line, and conditions, we were astonished that this episode in local investigative history was found to be infused with irony. Each discovery gave us pause and wonderment. What was also apparent during our conversations was that Dennis' own recollections from his Dayton youth and his unique perspective as a homicide detective demanded that he be folded into the story.

Judith and I found his role to have ironic twists as well ... as you will see. Read on.

—*Steve Grismer*

PROLOGUE
CHRISTMAS WEEK 1992

The 1992 Christmas holidays are celebrated inside an active Dayton Arcade.
Shoppers enter the walkway from Third Street as policemen stand guard.

The Dayton Arcade
(right)

West Third Street Entrance
across from
Court House Square

Shoppers *(below)* on
the mezzanine level
of the Arcade in 1992

"HollyDays" (above) framed on the elevator

"Holly Days!" Dayton, Ohio

The joy of the approaching holiday weekend envelops the good citizens of this declining Ohio town. Despite Dayton being a major industrial city with rustbelt woes, its Court House Square is festive this week. Children look in awe at its colorful, marvelously lighted tree.

Rekindled is the happiness of shoppers anticipating seasonal fare and shared times with family and friends.

Directly across the street, people circulate the boutiques and eateries inside the Arcade Square. The crowd mingles

while the Dayton Philharmonic performs. Orchestra instruments glisten from the reflective sunshine filtering through the vast Arcade glass rotunda.

Built in 1902, the historical local landmark is bustling with renewed energy.

In spite of its grandeur, the Arcade struggled in the 1970s, was bankrupt by 1984, and had closed to a fading public in 1990. But now it has temporarily reopened for the 1992 Christmas season as ...

"HollyDays!"

Dennis Murphy grew up in the "Gem City" and eventually joined the Dayton police force. He remembers the efforts made by municipal officials to revitalize the city center.

Officer Dennis Murphy

DENNIS: "Police Chief James Newby had recently formed a police mounted patrol unit. Kids and adults absolutely loved the horses. It was a definite draw for downtown.

"The holiday spirit was enhanced even more by the unusually warm weather … bright days; mild temperatures in the mid-40s … heavy sweater weather for many people who are used to much colder.

Chief James Newby

"I remember the early week was pleasant, even with the darkness of winter solstice arriving on Monday."

Winter Fun - Kids drawn to the horse ridden by Mounted Patrolman Tim Zimmer

But early darkness and the longest nights of the year foreshadow other changes in the advancing week. By Wednesday, warmth gives way to freezing temperatures. Jarring winds blow in darkening clouds and bitter cold ... 35-mile-per-hour gusts drive festivities for many indoors. The cold keeps people inside... but some, especially the young, are not deterred from roaming about.

In one poor corner of the city, a small band of youths are emboldened by a 16-year-old runaway girl who just joined their group – Laura Taylor. She is an encouraging influence among her teenage companions ... all of whom are estranged from family, disengaged from social norms ... adrift.

She instantly takes a liking to 19-year-old Marvallous Keene. He hangs with this group on and off, having separated for a time to move to the west coast where his father lives.

Though a former church choirboy, Taylor's new boyfriend is a menacing-looking figure. In fact, he boasts that he became a Crips gang member when in California. Taylor, Keene and the other teens, who will soon fancy themselves a local gang – the self-proclaimed Downtown Posse – wander in the underbelly of society, set apart by depravity, adolescent volatility ...

... and prone to impulsive thrills.

Chapter 1

CHRISTMAS EVE

2012 The Moraine Embassy Bar & Grill, 25 S. Ludlow Street in Downtown Dayton
The Embassy was "the place" for newspaper reporters, court employees and cops.

–Photograph courtesy of Elizabeth Weeks

Orgy on Prescott Avenue

Thursday – It is Chrismas Eve and these teens crave excitement ... something taboo.

At Taylor's suggestion, she, Keene, and another drifter, Heather Mathews, leave their hangout, an apartment belonging to their friend, Bill McIntyre. His home is in public housing at 159 Yuma Place, a two-story row apartment in a west-end Dayton View neighborhood – Edgewood Court.

It is the early morning hours, and once mild air is now frigid and in the upper teens. Despite biting winds, the group walks three miles from Bill's place to 3321 Prescott Avenue. There lives a local General Motors machine operator who moved to Dayton from Detroit four years earlier. He will be home this holiday weekend.

Even though it is 4 a.m., they knock on the front door to the house in which 34-year-old Joseph Wilkerson resides. Taylor is eager to prove to her companions that she can entice her friend Joe to invite them inside his warm home by the prospect of an orgy.

Recognizing the young girl at his door, Joe allows the three shivering youths inside.

Three hours later, tired from the partying and their long, cold walk to Joe's house, they leave with Christmas presents but must use one of Joe's two cars, a 1974 red Buick Electra, to take the gifts home. About 7 a.m., they return to Yuma Place.

Scheming for Cash

After a brief respite, Taylor and Keene head downtown to Arcade Square. It's one of the few active places that belie the decline of downtown Dayton, a city still reeling from the economic hardship of the 1980s.

DENNIS: "Dayton had problems because of the public's growing apprehension of the conditions in the center of the city.

"I had just graduated from Belmont High School the year before and was well aware of how the troubles were compounded by a Dayton Public School District decision.

Dennis Murphy,
12th Grade,
Belmont High School

"The district chose to shed a fleet of school buses in favor of contracting services with the local public bus service.

"And the transfer point for high school students was at the hub of town, the Old Court House at Third and Main Streets. Teenagers frequently gathered there in concentrated numbers and at the nearby Arcade.

"The congregating of school kids meant there was trouble almost on a daily basis.

"It was a problem that persisted long after I had entered law enforcement with Dayton Police"

Christmas Season at the Old Court House

Foot patrol, bicycle patrol, and the mounted patrolmen are often used to deter criminal behavior outside.

The advantage of the mounted patrol is that observant officers rise above a crowd. Unfortunately, the horses cannot patrol the interior Arcade where troublemaking teens slip in among the crowds.

Mounted Patrol Sergeants
Scott Stimmel & Bruce Burt

Taylor and Keene mingle with last minute holiday shoppers inside. While soaking in the atmosphere, they panhandle in the desire for quick cash. But without any immediate gratification, Taylor thinks of ways to use her body to attract a score.

She and Keene meet up at the Broaster Hut on North Main Street with Heather Mathews' new boyfriend, 17-year old Demarcus Smith. The three relax and talk a little. Taylor recalls the wild time they had earlier that morning at Joe's house on Prescott. Whispering inside the restaurant, they

devise a robbery scheme and then head into the winter cold.

Meandering on the near street corner well worn by hookers, Taylor angles for a sucker. She finds one. She gestures a trick and jumps into his warm car. Circling from Great Miami Boulevard onto Neal Avenue, they

The Broaster Hut at 865 North Main Street

quickly pull alongside the curb. Suddenly, the driver sees two threatening characters emerge from an old red Electra and approach him on foot.

Neal Avenue entering at 901 North Main Street

Cautious not to get too close themselves, Keene and Smith draw guns from their pockets.

In terror, the target slams the accelerator to escape. The armed would-be thieves fire two bullets through the car's back window, not the least bit concerned that it is still occupied by Taylor.

Frantically, the driver speeds away with Taylor inside the car. At first chance, she jumps free from the moving vehicle, but Taylor is unharmed in this shoddy hold-up attempt. Their easy mark flees for his life to a Dayton police station. Taylor is picked up by her accomplices.

This incident foreshadows a series of events unlike any experienced by Dayton police investigators.

Shortly after the failed robbery attempt, the body of a young lady, barely holding onto life, lies crumpled beneath a pay phone mounted on an outside wall of a store. The building is on a residential street in the Five Oaks neighborhood of northwest Dayton.

Thus begins a succession of crimes transcending age, gender, race, and ethnicity of both perpetrators and victims that will be forever remembered by those who investigated the crimes.

"You need to keep all your options open."
HOMICIDE SQUAD CALL OUT

It is **2012**. Across from the Arcade, the Moraine Embassy bar and grill is open to those who the owners call friends.

DENNIS: "The Embassy was 'the place' to go. Owned since 1969 by three Greek brothers from the old country, The Embassy was the watering hole in downtown Dayton for newspaper reporters, court employees and cops.

"Sadly, it was recently torn down but for years it was a place of comfort and conversation for many patrons."

The Embassy entrance on Ludlow

It has been 20 years since an evening in 1992 when four members of the Dayton police homicide squad were called out on Christmas Eve.

Now retired they reunite this day at The Embassy to recount a 40-hour holiday horror that unfolded for them beginning with a murder they are called to investigate.

40 HOURS / 0:00:01...
HRS:MINS:SECS

The detectives remember this Christmas Eve callout was initially not unlike any other notification received from police dispatch of a potential homicide.

Uniformed patrol officers are dispatched to 517 Neal Avenue. They respond to the scene and locate a victim with multiple gunshot wounds. They notify medics who remove the victim with life-threatening injuries to Grandview Hospital.

As the officers cordon off the area and search for witnesses, the on-scene sergeant requests the dispatcher send an evidence crew and contact the homicide squad. Sergeant Larry Grossnickle is notified.

Sgt. Grossnickle (left), Detectives Wade Lawson, Tom Lawson & Doyle Burke
Reunited in 2012 at *The Embassy*, remembering a "40-hour holiday horror"

Retired Dayton Police Homicide Sergeant Larry Grossnickle

LARRY: "We train ourselves to go out on these things and not to prejudge anything we see because it may take you down the wrong trail. You need to keep all your options open, especially when you don't have anything."

Retired Dayton Police Homicide Detective Wade Lawson

WADE: "We were used to receiving callouts just about on a daily basis and it was just another shooting. We didn't know it was a homicide at the time we got the call."

Memories of the callout are of an innocent woman, alone in the dark on Christmas Eve. It is 10:10 p.m. The victim's name: Danita Gullette. The lead detective: Wade Lawson.

WADE: "And we found this lady who had been shot.... We just had another murder and really had nothing to go on. No reason.... it just boggles one's mind. Gullette on the phone.

"They didn't walk up and say 'Here's a gun give me what you've got....' "

Danita is 18 years old. A single mother of a two-year-old toddler, she works while also attending school. She has very little money on her; nothing of any real value, except maybe to the eyes of vicious thieves. Uniformed officers notice her feet are shoeless, oddly exposed on the cold concrete surface.

When the detectives arrive on the shooting scene at Neal and Rockwood Avenues, Danita had been removed by medics to the Grandview emergency room, a mere five blocks away.

WADE: "We were surprised at the number of casings. I think she was hit maybe 5 times."

As with any shooting, the homicide unit initiates an investigation. There are nine bullet casings on the ground ... odd, because the Blazer aluminum casings, found mixed in pools of blood, are the type of ammunition typically used for target shooting.

By the time the detectives conduct their crime scene search, Danita had perished from multiple .25 caliber gunshot wounds.

She had been fatally struck in the chest and stomach as well as in the left thigh, right arm and left hand. Whatever defensive posture she took, she had no chance.

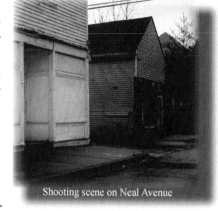
Shooting scene on Neal Avenue

WADE: "Well it's hard to know, at this point, with what we know.... We had no idea. One suspect? Two, three, four, five? We had no idea.

"All we knew is we had a homicide."

Though the investigators talk to few witnesses that night, they learn that three teens – one a petite, young girl – had run from Neal, north on Rockwood in the middle of the street. Passing a neighbor, the girl had cursed her as the gang of three rushed into the darkness.

It appears to be a random murder.

40 HOURS / 1:16:32...
HRS:MINS:SECS

"We shot her!"

While the detectives work the Gullette case and the coroner investigator examines the crime scene, Taylor, Keene and Smith are on the move.

They return to Bill's apartment at 159 Yuma Place to party with other friends: Mathews, Nick Woodson, age 16, Marvin Washington, 18, and his 16-year-old girlfriend, Wendy Cottrill.

Taylor, Keene and Smith are animated and voice their excitement for all to hear.

"We shot her! We shot her!"

Dayton woman shot

A Dayton woman was shot six or seven times in the abdomen and chest Thursday night in an alley behind 517 Neal Ave., police said. The victim, whose name was not released, was being treated at Grandview Hospital and Medical Center. Police learned of the shooting as they responded to a disturbance call at 10:30 p.m. Police Sgt. Jesse Hines III said investigators had no motive or suspects in the shooting.

Dayton Daily News article

1:20:07...
Hrs:Mins:Secs

It's 11:30 p.m. Even after the long day roaming the streets of Dayton, the gang's adrenalin flows as they revel. Suddenly, Mathews' ex-boyfriend, Jeffrey Wright, in a fit of jealousy, bursts through the door and crashes the Yuma party. He's searching for her.

Wright is quickly confronted by Demarcus Smith, Mathews' current boyfriend. The two teens get into a heated argument.

Enraged, Smith pulls his gun. As Jeffrey tears out of the apartment into the courtyard, Smith repeatedly fires at the panicked runner who manages to escape the courtyard but is badly injured. Having struck him four times, Smith has reason to believe Jeffrey is dying if not dead.

Despite the chaos, the gang realizes the sound of gunfire may soon have the Yuma courtyard crawling with cops as it is only one block away from the Fifth District Police Station.

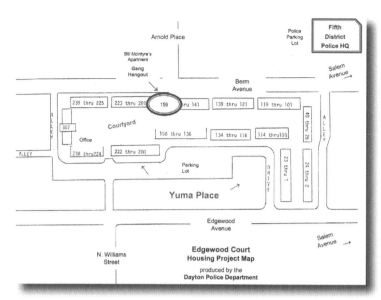

Edgewood Court
Housing Project Map
produced by the
Dayton Police Department

They mull over ideas for other places where they might disappear if Bill's place draws the police. Woodson offers his aunt's house at 729 Kumler Avenue where his cousin Deon lives. They settle on the house as a backup plan, but for now they stay at Yuma.

Woodson's offer of refuge now makes him the bona fide "fifth wheel" of the Downtown Posse.

2:07:58...

HRS:MINS:SECS

Holiday gives no break from crime

By Anna Caarley
DAYTON DAILY NEWS

Shootings and robberies over Christmas Eve and Christmas Day left a Dayton woman without presents for her family, a Domino's pizza delivery person without spare money and a Dayton man shot four times, authorities said.

Willie West, 55, of 767 Goodlow Ave. came home after midnight Thursday to find her presents opened and empty boxes stacked in her living room, police said.

Missing gifts included silk shirts, sweaters, a stereo, remote control car and toy truck... apparently entered the ...ng a bedroom window.

...ia driver had made a de-
...a Drive and Rustic Road
...day when he was ap-
...en who knocked on his
...e said.

...stan Stumn, told the
...ve any left. One of the
...a semiautomatic hand-
...d, police said, and demand-
...d money. Stumn handed over $40.

Shootings and robberies over Christmas Eve and Christmas Day left a Dayton woman without presents for her family, a Domino's pizza delivery person without spare money and a Dayton man shot four times, authorities said.

CHAPTER 2

CHRISTMAS

December 25, 1992: The front page of the Dayton Daily News

The **spirit of Christmas** is shared with the Dayton community.
Dayton Daily News - December 25, 1992

"It was Christmas night!"

Friday – The early morning of Christmas day is as blustery and icy as the day before. The group wakes up at Bill's apartment on Yuma Place with renewed spirit and energy.

Dayton Public Housing

They leave the confines of Edgewood Court to head back to Joe Wilkerson's house on Prescott Avenue.

8:50:32...
HRS:MINS:SECS

After a second but brief visit at Joe's place, Taylor, Keene, Smith and Woodson return to Bill's apartment for a while before heading over to the Kumler house. There they find a noontime Christmas meal of turkey and collard greens that Woodson's aunt had prepared before she left to visit family.

Off to the side, while proudly sporting Fila gym shoes her boyfriend, Demarcus Smith, had been wearing, Mathews confides to Woodson's girlfriend, Melissa Gomez.

The pay phone in the Neal Avenue alley

Mathews tells her the gang had stolen the shoes from a woman they killed in an alley at a pay phone the night before. Astonished, Gomez listens and says little.

Though Woodson's aunt is in the dark, the gang's impulsive bragging has widened around those in their circle to include partying pals Woodson, Washington, Cottrill, as well as Bill McIntyre... and, now, Melissa Gomez.

14:17:07...
HRS:MINS:SECS

The group spends the yuletide celebrating, but throughout the day they discuss potential sources for fast cash. Taylor, Keene, Smith and Mathews pack into Joe's red Electra, returning a third time to his house to continue their festivities on this cold Christmas day.

At the Prescott home, they take full advantage of the food and beverage Joe's place offers. While enjoying their fill of cupcakes and soda pop, and with Joe in the backroom, they scheme for easy money.

Taylor tells the group that her ex-boyfriend, Richmond Maddox, lives two blocks away on Larkspur Drive. She seizes upon the idea of luring him away from his house with the promise of hotel sex and then robbing him.

As early darkness approaches yet again this week of winter solstice, Taylor twice visits his nearby home but Richmond shows no interest in her advances.

21:20:00...
HRS:MINS:SECS

What to do? At 7:30 p.m., the four decide to split up using Joe's second car; Taylor and Keene drive his blue Grand Am, while the other two leave in the red Electra.

Christmas lights line and adorn downtown Dayton's Main Street at night.

Taylor and Keene drive to an ATM on Germantown Street with the intent of targeting a customer. Preoccupied, however, by their own compulsion to engage in sex, they squander a chance to rob a customer who approaches the "Green Machine."

Undaunted by the missed opportunity, the two drive off to meet up with Smith and Mathews. They know that automated banking machines are readily available targets throughout the city and can be easily stalked when they have nothing more lucrative. In fact, these four will later lurk in the shadows of an ATM on Salem.

RETIRED DAYTON POLICE HOMICIDE DETECTIVE TOM LAWSON

TOM: "This foursome set on the ATM machine ... and their goal was the next person, ... after they get their money, they would kill them.

"Not gonna rob them. [The gang] will kill them....

"It was Christmas night!"

"Maybe we will have a little Christmas after all."
2ND HOMICIDE SQUAD CALL OUT

Coming up empty-handed on Germantown, and relentless in her pursuit of Richmond Maddox, Taylor is dropped off alone at his house while the gang lurks nearby.

She knocks on his door. This time he gives in to her.

22:40:23...
HRS:MINS:SECS

Soon Richmond and Taylor are in his car. She cozies up to him, and the two take off with him behind the wheel.

Driving across Salem into a residential neighborhood, Richmond realizes a car is ominously following them. He senses something is very wrong.

Taylor tries to reassure him that it is her family in the other car, but Richmond panics, accelerating onto Benton Drive.

Suddenly Taylor pulls a Derringer and, with cruel abruptness, fires one scorching bullet into Richmond's head, causing his auto to ram and then ricochet off a parked car.

Taylor jumps out of the moving vehicle right before it slams into a tree.

Keene and Smith furiously try to pull Richmond's lifeless body from the wreckage hoping to steal his car as Taylor limps two blocks to the Miracle Lane Shopping Center. She's picked up by Mathews in the red Electra. Frenzied, Taylor howls to Mathews, "I shot him in the head. I shot him!"

Miracle Lane, mere blocks from Benton murder scene

Meanwhile, Keene and Smith, fearing discovery, abandon the dying victim and hustle to their waiting car. They rush to their Yuma hangout where they feel they will go unnoticed, at least for the time being.

Having heard the crash, residents in the quiet neighborhood of Benton Avenue call the police.

The initial responding uniformed officers believe this is a critical-injury accident. But when Richmond is removed by ambulance to Good Samaritan Hospital, closer examination by medical personnel reveals a more sinister circumstance.

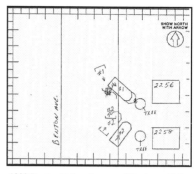

1992 Dayton Police diagram of Benton collision

23:30:46...

HRS:MINS:SECS

As a sequel to Christmas Eve, the homicide squad is called out Christmas night.

WADE: "We got a call of a dead body on Benton, and I recall very well we got there and a car was into a tree. And first it was thought to be just a traffic accident.... So they removed him to the hospital and found that he had a .32 caliber bullet in his head."

The detectives have no reason to believe the murder of Maddox has any connection to any other crime. The professionals complete their grim business this Friday night but feel the successive nights of murder are an aberration. They are hopeful and imagine this weekend will herald a customary, peaceful holiday respite for them and their families.

Detective Doyle Burke *(far right)* and fellow members of the Homicide Squad

Retired Dayton Police Homicide Detective Doyle Burke

DOYLE: "We had gone home at that time feeling pretty dumb, fat and happy."

WADE: "But we feel pretty good at this point. We think, 'You know, ... maybe we will have a little Christmas after all.' "

"There's a lot done behind the scenes..."

Though the four homicide investigators are accustomed to the exhaustive routine, they had had little sleep. They had been investigating an unrelated murder from Tuesday, worked their regular shift the next day, and were off-duty just a few hours when called out on Christmas Eve for Gullette's murder at the pay phone. That investigation had stretched into the early morning hours. Finally able to return home, they attempted to sleep.

With restless thoughts, and after only a few hours in bed, they had risen to show for their morning roll call, working all Christmas day before going home. But after only a few hours, they received the late evening callout for the killing on Benton... their third homicide in four days.

As a homicide detective, Dennis knows the difficulties investigators face.

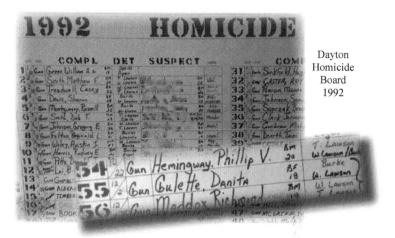

Dayton
Homicide
Board
1992

Active-duty Dayton Police Detective Dennis Murphy,
Homicide Squad 2009-2016

DENNIS: "When I was assigned to the homicide squad,
I learned from Sergeant Gary White and Detective
Doyle Burke how to investigate crime scenes. But I also
discovered there's a lot done behind the scenes, and that would have been the same in 1992.

2 holiday shootings raise city's homicide count to 56 this year

: Dayton shootings over the holiday left two people dead, raising Dayton's homicide count to 56 this year, authorities said.
A 19-year-old man died at Good Samaritan Hospital and Health Center on Friday night, a hospital spokesman said.
The man, whose name was withheld pending notification of family, crashed his car into a parked car in front of 2256 Ben-

Dayton police were also investigating the death of Danita Gullette, 18, who died Thursday night after being shot about seven times in the stomach.
Gullette of 709 Five Oaks Ave. was shot in an alley behind 517 Neal Ave. about 10:15 p.m. Christmas Eve, said Dayton police Sgt. Jesse Hines III.
Police had no suspects and did not know the motive of the shooting.
...died at Grandview ...nd Medical Center at ...said medical super-...k Large.

"As time allowed, witnesses from all these murder cases were interviewed, handwritten observations and investigative notes were recorded into official reports, police records were

Dennis Murphy with Tom Lawson

checked, other potential witnesses were sought, and leads were run down by the detectives.

DENNIS: "At the same time, investigators were hampered by the four-day holiday.

"Even as they pressed forward to solve these crimes, they had to await the reopening of offices and the Monday-morning return of civilian employees for forensic analysis, coroner examinations, and other essential support."

Teenage Stalkers

While the detectives seek clues to Richmond Maddox's murder on Benton, the teenage stalkers hunt for an easy victim to rob.

26:50:17...
HRS:MINS:SECS

Taylor, Keene, Smith, and Mathews settle into Joe's blue Grand Am while Woodson, with his cousin Deon Pinson and two others from the gang, get into Joe's red Electra. The two cars travel to East Dayton but no easy mark is found. Sometime around one in the morning, the cars get separated.

The red Electra – with Woodson, Pinson and others inside – pulls into an industrial area near Beckel and East Third Streets. Because they are traveling in a desolate area in darkness and breaking curfew, the teenage occupants draw the suspicion of a patrolling Dayton police crew.

As the police maneuver to stop the Electra, the nervous juveniles attempt to flee but find themselves trapped in a blind alley. They are apprehended. A short time later, however, the teenagers are all freed from detention.

Glad to be released to the home of his mother on Limestone Avenue, Woodson does not realize at this point that he will come to rely on police for his safety a few short hours later.

Meanwhile, Taylor, Keene, Smith and Mathews travel in the blue Grand Am to a bank on Salem, again with plans to rob a "Green Machine" customer. Having immersed themselves in acts of depravity for nearly 24 hours, they fall asleep in the car ...exhausted.

29:20:43...
HRS:MINS:SECS

Soon detectives would come to learn the predatory nature of this posse of thugs.

Blind alleys in the factory neighborhood of East Third and Beckel Streets

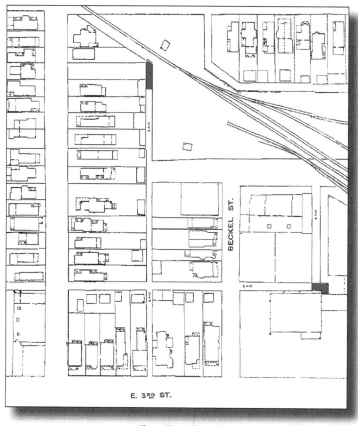

CHAPTER 3

DAY AFTER CHRISTMAS
(Morning)

The Short Stop Mini Market, 1212 West Fifth Street

–Photograph courtesy of retired Sgt. Roger Edwards

Montgomery County Sheriff BP robbery Investigation No 92-361-052

SUPPLEMENTARY OFFENSE REPORT
SHERIFF'S OFFICE

ORIGINAL MASTER NO.
92-361-052

OFFENSE Sig. 3   SERIAL NO.

COMPLAINANT

ADDRESS   Malvern Ave., Dayton, Ohio

45406

Additional details of offense, Progress of Investigation, etc.

PLACE OF OCCURRENCE: 3898 Salem Ave., BP Station, Harrison Twp., Montgomery County, Ohio

SUSPECT INFORMATION:

1. B/M 5'11", 210 lbs., black/brown

2. B/M 5'10", 155 lbs., black/brown

VEHICLE OBTAINED:

A 1988 Dodge Shadow, black in color, Ohio registration FMB 186.

SYNOPSIS OF CRIME:

On 12-26-92, at 0718 hrs., the above complainant was in the parking lot of 3898 Salem Ave., BP Station, Harrison Twp., Montgomery County. The complainant was approached by the above suspects, with one brandishing a small hand gun and threatening bodily harm to the complainant. The suspects then left in the complainant's vehicle, proceeding southbound on Salem Avenue.

INVESTIGATION:

On 12-26-92, this Officer received the above complaint for review and follow up investigation.

Upon reviewing the reports as submitted, it was noted that on 12-26-92, at approximately 0721 hrs., Dep. J. Randolph # 1218, Crew # 242, was dispatched to 3898 Salem Ave., BP Station, on the report of an Aggravated Robbery.

Upon arrival, Dep. Randolph contacted the complainant and she advised of the following information. At approximately 0718 hrs., she had pulled her vehicle, which is registered in her husband's name, up to the air station in order to place some air into her tire. The complainant advised that she had exited her vehicle and was on the right front passenger side of her vehicle, at which time she was approached by a B/M subject, who had walked from a dark blue colored vehicle, being parked by the pay phone. The complainant advised that one of the B/M's walked about halfway between the suspect vehicle and her vehicle, while the other B/M

SIGNED DEP. J. H. CASS # 1119

"You will die today!"

Saturday – It is a freezing 9° outside ... the coldest day of the week. The group wakes up in the blue Grand Am early in the morning darkness.

32:20:38...
HRS:MINS:SECS

They focus their attention on the "Green Machine" on Salem for the second time, still finding no success.

TOM: "[They] set ... up on Salem Avenue all night long and several hours and ... the next person that uses that machine ... gonna rob them ... and take what they've got.

ATM "Green Machine"

"And no one used the machine."

And so, the gang takes a different tact. They head to a BP station in the county on Salem. There, the gang spots a young woman pumping air into her tires. As Keene and Smith burst from their car, Keene pulls a silver gun and points it at the woman, yelling:

"You will die today!"

In terror, the woman flees for her life as the muggers jump into her black Dodge Shadow, speeding away. She runs inside the gas station. The Montgomery County Sheriff's Department is immediately called. The victim, narrowly escaping her murder, reports her car stolen in a robbery.

TOM: "This went ... to literally joy killings. No more than steal a car and take a joyride. And they were into it. They were enjoying it."

Now both cars – the black Dodge Shadow with Keene and Smith and the blue Grand Am carrying Taylor and Mathews – head to Kumler where they leave behind one car. The gang still has no cash but is undeterred. They're on the move.

33:08:57...

HRS:MINS:SECS

Sgt. Moises Perez

At the Dayton Police Signal Building, dispatch sergeant Moises Perez is assigning crews to respond to a routine prowler call in the Fifth District:

PEREZ: "Are there any crews that can head that way?"

CREW 515: "I can head that way."

PEREZ: "Okay, [Crew] 515."

CREW 522B: "[Crew] 522B, I can head that way."

PEREZ: "Okay, I've got two crews assigned. Anybody else that can head that way, go ahead. It's now 7:25."

But then Sgt. Perez suspends his transmission to issue an "all-points bulletin" to Dayton crews.

PEREZ: "All crews, also be advised, the County just had an armed robbery at Salem and Free Pike. Car was taken at gunpoint... black male suspect... 1989 Shadow."

"No one was safe."
3RD HOMICIDE SQUAD CALL OUT

Now three miles from the BP station, the gang makes a quick decision. Keene and Smith insist that in order to get the cash they want, they need to rob a store – a solid, more reliable target.

Mathews takes the wheel of the black Dodge Shadow and gives a .25 caliber Raven Arms semi-automatic gun to Smith.

33:10:26...
HRS:MINS:SECS

Taylor chooses the target, the Short Stop Mini Market on West Fifth Street.

Pulling in front of the store, the plan is hatched. Taylor will walk into the market. If she doesn't emerge within a few minutes, it's the sign that the coast is clear for the hold up.

Taylor enters the store to case it.

Short Stop Mini Market on West Fifth Street

The counter inside the Short Stop Market

Behind the counter is Sarah Abraham, a 38-year old divorced mother of three small children, the oldest 11.

Hardworking, Sarah and her family bought the small store from the previous owner and opened their own market eight years earlier after she emigrated from Ethiopia.

Taylor asks Sarah how much a soft drink costs. Taylor is five cents short of the price. A regular store customer, 71-year old Jimmy Thompson, offers the innocent-looking, young girl a nickel. Taylor accepts it and then wanders around the store.

A few minutes pass. Suddenly, Keene and Smith burst into the store, demanding money. Sarah opens the register but can produce only $40. Keene snatches it from her hands and then, in cold-blooded fashion, shoots the young store-owner in the face and head.

Just as quickly, Smith fires his .25 caliber pistol at the two other people in the store, Thompson – who instantly collapses over the counter – and Jones Pettus, who suffers a terrible bullet wound to the stomach.

33:17:19...
HRS:MINS:SECS

While the gang flees, a witness to the shooting calls the fire department for an ambulance. The fire dispatcher, in turn, transmits the shooting to Sgt. Perez. Again, the sergeant stops in the middle of his dispatch:

Perez: "Okay, stand by there just a minute...."

Seated at the dispatch console, Sgt. Perez presses a foot pedal that engages the microphone to broadcast to the crew and simultaneously pushes a button to emit a "tone." The familiar high-pitched sound broadcasted over the radio alerts officers of life-threatening circumstances and to respond to the scene with lights and sirens engaged.

Perez: "[Crews] 322 and 326. Start for 1201 West Fifth... shots fired. Fire [department]'s getting [an emergency call of an incident] as a shooting. Go ahead and make a check and advise. Fifth and Williams [Streets], 1201 West Fifth [Street]."

Crew 322: "Okay. We're [headed] out there."

In mere moments, Sgt. Perez makes clear the situation the officers will encounter.

Perez: "[Crews] 322 and 326, [it's] definitely a shooting."

Crew 322: "Clear." (a police siren wails in the background)

Within two minutes, the first crew arrives at the Mini Market and advises of the grim circumstances.

Crew 322: "[Crew] 320 (calling for the street sergeant), ... head this way. This may be a head shot."

Crew 320: "I'm on the way. Clear."

Crew 322: Yeah, we got two shot."

Crew 320: "Clear."

While the fire medics do their best to stabilize the victims for removal, the officers spend the next half hour trying to make sense of the brutality at the Mini Market.

Police Evidence
Technician
outside the Mini
Market *(above).*

Polaroid photographs
taken at the crime
scene and placed in the
Investigation Case File

They interview people nearby, determine the scope of the crime scene, and identify the location of evidence. Now, the routine crime scene investigation notification process begins.

CREW 322: "[Crew] 322 [to] Dispatch. For your information, … the female shot is extremely critical. Removing to Saint E's [Hospital] now. The man is, uh, stable. He will be removed to Saint E's. We have no suspect information or witnesses show up."

PEREZ: "Okay, did you want an E-crew (evidence technician) to start that way also?"

(slight pause)

PEREZ: "[Crew] 322. Uh, we've got an E-crew that we can send to you if you need it."

CREW 322: "Yeah, we're going to need that.… They were shot inside the building."

PEREZ: "Okay, we'll put [the E-crew] out (i.e. assigned to process the crime scene)."

Sgt. Perez advises the evidence crew to respond to the Mini Market so the technician can gather evidence, lift latent fingerprints, take photographs, and diagram the crime scene.

The street sergeant, having grasped the full nature of the crimes committed, makes the obvious decision to request the homicide detectives to respond to the scene.

CREW 320: "[Crew] 320 [to] Dispatch. Go ahead and notify the detectives. Apparently, this was in the process of a robbery."

PEREZ: "Okay sir. 8:09."

As with all life-threatening shooting incidents, the homicide squad is briefed and summoned by the dispatcher for the third time in less than 34 hours.

Tom: "Doyle got that call. Wade and I were working that same day we were all there processing the scene of it. And very, very sad.

"Sarah Abraham was a sweet lady, owned the store, everybody in the neighborhood loved her. She was kind and tried to help everyone out.... A senseless killing...."

34:15:31...
Hrs:Mins:Secs

The store is a horrendous scene. Blood is splattered on display cases and saturates the surface rugs. Aluminum bullet casings litter the floor.

The detectives learn that Sarah has been rushed to the hospital where she lingers for five days until the family has her removed from life support.

Thompson had feigned being shot, escaping unharmed. Pettus, a regular store customer, has been struck but was fortunate to survive his gunshot wounds.

Tom: "We got the shell casings at the scene and we got the fellow Jones Pettus who ... was working in the store and he was shot. And he was a big help to us later. The robbery and the fleeing, with the cars and the shell casings.... It started to make a little more sense."

Doyle: "There was Blazer ammunition, .25 caliber Blazer.... Sarah basically gave them everything they wanted and they still killed her."

WADE: "These are some dangerous people. They need to be caught and they need to be caught in a hurry."

DOYLE: "Our concern really was the capture. Whoever it was, however many there were; this was a series of senseless killings. No one was safe.... The capture was of paramount importance."

🛡 🛡 🛡 🛡

Paranoia Setting In

Having pilfered a pittance from the Mini Market, Taylor, Keene, Smith and Mathews search for Nick Woodson, who only six hours earlier had been apprehended by police with three others in East Dayton and had since been released from custody. They find him at his mother's Limestone Avenue home near Germantown Street in West Dayton.

34:25:44...
HRS:MINS:SECS

It now dawns on this collection of treacherous miscreants that they might get caught for their deadly crimes. In only two days they have threatened to shoot or actually fired gun shots at numerous innocent people, believing they killed at least four.

News headline post-killings

This core group is now worried that their friends know too much and are likely to squeal so they huddle to talk.

Smith is convinced that someone has already snitched to the police and swears, "We ought to unload a clip in [his] ass." Overhearing their muted conversation, Woodson senses that he may be one they suspect. It is not an unfounded fear.

WADE: "I know that they had … more people that they intended to kill that day.

"And that was out of the mouth of Marvallous Keene, looking you in the eyes, and telling [you]…, 'Yes, we were gonna kill Nick Woodson….' "

Urgency to Find Killers

The detectives investigating the Short Stop Mini Market shootings now believe that the crimes of the weekend are not isolated events but are connected based on physical evidence.

WADE: "Things began to change as we began to see more of what was going on…. We were actually working pretty much around the clock … that was a tough weekend, wasn't it?"

DOYLE: "It was chaotic, I mean we're used to chaos, it's all we deal with, and this was chaotic even for us."

LARRY: "Something like that you can't let go on. It isn't that we [should] find them … it's we *have* to find them."

35:10:16…
HRS:MINS:SECS

Dayton Daily News Christmas weekend chronology

SHOOTINGS

■ **Dec. 24:** Danita Gullette shot seven times as she stood at a pay phone in the 500 block of Neal Avenue.
■ **Dec. 25:** Richmond T. Maddox of Larkspur Drive found dead in a wrecked car on Benton Avenue.
■ **Dec. 26:** Sarah Abraham, employee of Short-Stop Mini Market, 1201 W. Fifth St., and customer Jones Pettus shot during robbery.

"You wanna go for a ride?"

Before venturing out, fearing the cars might be spotted by the police, the gang switches license plates between the blue Grand Am and the black Dodge Shadow. The gang parks the blue car on Catalpa Drive, a short block away from Kumler.

It is a little after 9 a.m. Taylor, Keene, Smith and Mathews, along with a worried Woodson, head for Yuma Place in the Dodge Shadow. They pick up Wendy Cottrill and Marvin Washington, inviting them to get something to drink.

35:15:28...
HRS:MINS:SECS

WADE: "I think there was nine of them living in an apartment together.... They were just sitting home while the others were out running around and somebody says,

"'You know, they might call in and report us, we better just go pick them up....' So, they go to the apartment [and say,] 'Hey you. You wanna go for a ride?' 'Sure' ... And they get in the car."

Keene is at the wheel of the Shadow. The six others have crammed in the car with two of the girls sitting on their boyfriends' laps to fit inside. They travel to a beer and wine drive-thru and soon pass around Wild Irish Rose and Thunderbird wine while on the move.

But Nick Woodson is still nervous, wondering if he is the next target. He has to get out of that car. He asks to be dropped off at his mother's house on Limestone. Keene lets him out of the packed sedan and Woodson hurries into the house.

35:45:34...
HRS:MINS:SECS

A Place for Dead People

While on the move, the group continues drinking. Keene, in the haze of alcohol, becomes despondent thinking about the violent death of his older brother, Maurice, who was killed at the age of 19 while committing a robbery two years prior.

As his alcohol-induced thoughts deepen, Keene's despair turns into paranoia. He makes a brief stop at West Memory Gardens Cemetery to visit Maurice's grave.

–Photograph above courtesy of Carolyn J. Burns

The loneliness of the cemetery merely intensifies his feelings of desolation and, so, Keene decides to leave. He drives six miles from the Germantown Street gravesite toward town.

Declaring to the others that he has to take a leak, Keene maneuvers the car down Richley Avenue and turns into a desolate gravel yard across from Louise Troy School.

Viewed 10 miles from the gravel yard on Richley Avenue, the faint image of the Dayton skyline (below)

There is privacy here. The gravel pit is a barren, lonely place, and much quieter than the cemetery ... for the moment...

... and, then, gunshots fill the air.

35:55:17...
HRS:MINS:SECS

CHAPTER 4

DAY AFTER CHRISTMAS
(Afternoon)

The intersection of West Riverview and Kumler Avenues
Neighborhood of the self-proclaimed "Downtown Posse"

"It's coming together fast...."

In preparation for the deluge of press coverage sure to come, Sgt. Grossnickle must brief command personnel about the Short Stop Mini Market, the fourth shooting of the Christmas weekend.

He returns to the Dayton Safety Building on West Third Street – the police headquarters – while his homicide squad probes the fresh shooting scene a mere one mile away.

The Short Stop Mini Market crime reveals to the detectives an odd thread of coincidence that seems to tie the three recent killings... the suspicious presence of a brazen female teen at or close to the murders.

A petite female had reportedly fled from the market at the time of the shooting according to store employee accounts; an insolent girl had been witnessed by residents running down Neal Avenue on Christmas Eve; and, after having interviewed Maddox's family, the detectives learned that his ex-girlfriend may have been with him on the night of his brutal murder ... and that offers a significant lead.

Now, the detectives have a name and a person of interest to track down.

The normally peaceful holiday weekend is disrupted by alarming radio news broadcasts of the tragic Mini Market shootings, raising fears within the community. At the Dayton Police Signal Building, calls with tips are pouring in.

Soon, Woodson would be one of the callers.

37:20:53...
HRS:MINS:SECS

On Limestone, away from the others, Woodson ponders his fate, eventually deciding to seize the opportunity to contact police to save his own skin.

TOM: "And Nick Woodson, the reason he came forward is because he figured he was going be next."

LARRY: "Yeah, [Woodson] called me on the phone and he started telling me … he knew this and he knew that and he knew some stuff that nobody else knew."

DOYLE: "I mean, it's all coming together fast…."

Outside his mother's house, Woodson stresses over what to do … stay or leave.

He lays bare his predicament to a neighbor — that killers driving a black Dodge Shadow might come to the house to kidnap him. Alarmed, the neighbor rushes inside and, when he no longer sees Woodson outside, calls the police.

38:50:08...
HRS:MINS:SECS

AN A-P-B
"Attention all crews!"

Dayton police dispatch Sergeant Moises Perez is being fed information from the tips received and, in turn, transmits the broadcast from his position at the dispatch console.

One of the officers monitoring the dispatcher's radio traffic is uniform patrol Sergeant John Huber, Crew 520. This is his first day back to work after the holiday. He is trying to catch up with the

events of the last two days after roll

Dayton Police Dispatch Console

call. Early in his shift, Sgt. Huber heard a broadcast of the vehicle taken that morning in the BP robbery.

The time is now 1:41 p.m.

Sgt. Huber at Roll Call

39:31:12...
HRS:MINS:SECS

ALL-POINTS-BULLETIN

PEREZ: "Attention all crews. All crews, be on the lookout for possible homicide suspects. Looking for a four-door black Shadow, a four-door black Shadow.

"One of the occupants, a black male, has a red rag on his head. Accompanied by a white female, a black female, and three other black males.

Dispatch Radio Tower

PEREZ: "Possibly took someone against their will; another black male. Should be on the lookout for a four-door black Shadow, with five black males, a white female, and a black female.

Sergeant Perez

"It's definitely gonna be worth stopping them. Contact me or homicide squad."

PEREZ: "Also, we're looking for a small red car. Well, we were looking for these people. Supposedly changed from a small red car to a stolen [car], which is a four-door black Shadow... They hang around Summit Courts, Dayton View, and Edgemont neighborhoods. At 1341 hours." (1:41 p.m.)

Sgt. Huber decides to leave the Fifth District office with the intention of searching Dayton View for a Dodge Shadow. It is a vehicle common to the day's two seemingly unrelated robberies.

HUBER: "[Crew] 520 [to] Dispatch. I didn't write it down... (static) 1-8-6, a black Shadow that was taken in a robbery this morning at Salem and Free Pike. Do you happen to have that written down?"

Sergeant Huber

Recalling the earlier broadcast from the county involving the Salem BP carjacking, Officer Rick Blommel responds with the license plate number:

BLOMMEL: "Frank-Mary-Boston-1-8-6."

PEREZ: "At 1342. Also, the occupant's name is probably gonna be a Nicholas Woodson, [spelled] W-O-O-D-S-O-N. He's a black male. At 1342 hours." (1:42 p.m.)

"What do you mean, 'He's not here?'"

Unknown to Sgt. Perez, Nick Woodson – now acting out of panicked self-preservation – is speaking on the phone with Sgt. Grossnickle.

LARRY: "I called Wade and I said, 'Can you go by and pick him up at his house.' I had him on the phone still and I said, 'He'll be there to pick you up,' and he said, 'Okay.' "

The Lawson brothers head for Limestone to pick up their anxious new informant. He may know the teenage girl or offer clues as to the identities of the shooting suspects.

LARRY: "They got there in 10 minutes, not even that long I think, and they said 'He's not here.' And I said…'What do you mean he's not here? He told me he's going to be there!' "

Overcome with nerves, Woodson decided he could not wait. Needing a safe haven from where he was set loose, Woodson quickly disappears from Limestone before the gang reappears … or the detectives arrive.

39:36:19…
HRS:MINS:SECS

In the meantime, homicide detectives working multiple shootings transmit information about a person of interest over the radio.

Prompted by the call from Woodson to Sgt. Grossnickle, Det. Wade Lawson decides to broadcast information on the murder of Richmond Maddox the evening before:

W. LAWSON: "[Crew] 612 [to] Dispatch."

PEREZ: "[Crew] 612."

W. LAWSON: "Like to make a preliminary broadcast."

PEREZ: "Go right ahead."

W. LAWSON: "Wanted for questioning on the homicide from last night ... on Benton. Trying to locate a Laura, L-A-U-R-A, Taylor, T-A-Y-L-O-R. Black female, date of birth is 1-31-76. She's about five three, medium build, brown skin."

"Parents live at Genesee at Gettysburg. We made contact with them. She's been missing for about two and a half weeks... Was last seen wearing a red and black plaid long coat. If located, detain. Contact the Homicide Squad."

PEREZ: "End of broadcast at 1347." (1:47 p.m.)

39:37:21...
HRS:MINS:SECS

Having fled Limestone, Woodson returns to his aunt's house on Kumler but before he can leave, the gang suddenly returns with intentions of taking care of other business. And they have a target in mind.

Keene pulls the unnerved Woodson aside and tells him to kill his girlfriend, Melissa Gomez, "because she [knows] too much." Gripped with fear, Woodson agrees to do it.

"Frank-Mary-Boston 1-8-6"

In the meantime, Sgt. Huber is traveling westbound on West Riverview when he glances down Kumler. He spots a black Dodge facing south toward the dead end.

Driving down the street, he runs the plate number on his keyboard display terminal. The plate is registered to a Pontiac.

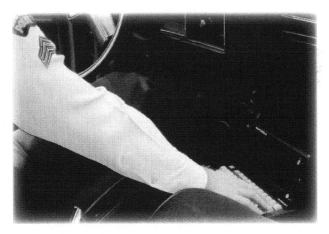

A 1992 In-car KDT Unit - Keyboard Display Terminal

The sergeant then turns right into the alley that runs two doors from 729 Kumler with a plan to swing around. He wants to better position himself to watch the Shadow.

As he circles out of the alley, Sgt. Huber sees a blue Pontiac Grand Am with no rear plate along the curb near the dead end of Catalpa. He exits his cruiser to obtain the vehicle identification number from the blue car. Peering through the Grand Am windshield, he quickly finds it on the dash board and writes it down. Then he spots a front license plate.

It is breathtakingly familiar: F-M-B-1-8-6.

39:38:18...
HRS:MINS:SECS

Leaving his patrol car parked on Catalpa, the sergeant looks for a way to stake out the black Shadow while keeping watch on the Grand Am. Then, he radios the dispatcher.

1990 Ford LTD Crown Victoria

HUBER: "[Do you have] another crew available? I've come across a car at the dead-end of Catalpa. It's got Frank-Mary-Boston-1-8-6 (FMB 186) on the front plate. There's a black Shadow that's one block over from me. It's parked with Frank-King-Dayton-7-2-7 (FKD 727) and the plates don't belong on it. I think the car's down here. I just want to get another crew in the area and maybe sit back on it."

PEREZ: "Okay. [Crew] 522?"

CREW 522: "At Cornell and Gettysburg."

PEREZ: "Get with [Crew] 520...."

On foot and dangerously exposed to suspects that have committed serious crimes at two places this day, Sgt. Huber analyzes the situation aloud to the dispatcher:

HUBER: "I've got a navy-blue Grand Am with the keys still in it. Driver's window is gone. No plate on the back. The front plate is Frank-Mary-Boston-1-8-6 (FMB 186). I think that's the one that was on that Shadow. About a block east from me, one block off Catalpa is a black Shadow, Frank-King-Dayton-7-2-7 (FKD 727)."

Strategically, Sgt. Huber decides to walk east into the cross alley. Concealing himself at the alley behind 729 Kumler he waits for suspects to appear and either cut through the yards to the Grand Am or drive the Shadow north to Riverview.

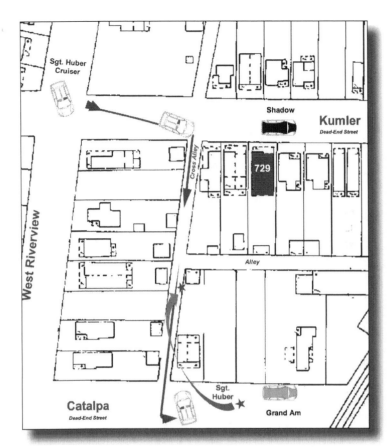

HUBER: "I'm gonna stick with the Grand Am, since I've already driven up on it. It's sitting here. The trunk's broken on it. It's probably gonna be stolen. Key's still in the ignition, but ... [Crew] 522, just watch this black Shadow. I think if he heads up... Kumler...."

PEREZ: (interjecting) "Okay, we've got to use extreme caution, 'cause these guys are all wanted for shootings, probably two of 'em. Maybe a possible homicide, too. At 1350 hours." (1:50 p.m.)

39:40:47...
HRS:MINS:SECS

W. LAWSON: "[Crew] 612 to 520."

HUBER: "[Crew] 520, go ahead."

W. LAWSON: (transmission cut out by another crew) "...and the year of the Grand Am."

HUBER: "It's navy blue, it's a newer one. The key was in it; doesn't belong in it, anyway. The driver's side window's gone. The steering column has been peeled."

W. LAWSON: "Is that a two-door or four-door?"

HUBER: "It's a two-door."

W. LAWSON: "Clear."

HUBER: "[Crew] 612 ... there is a black Shadow, though, that I think was the one stolen earlier this morning in an armed robbery [in the county].

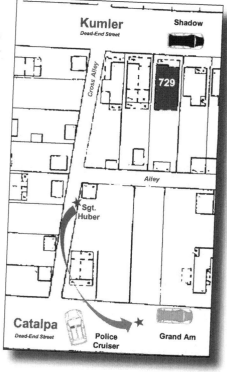

"It's parked, I think, a block over. I'm gonna go back by real fast. Make sure it hasn't moved."

W. LAWSON: "Clear. We're on Germantown; we are heading in that direction."

Detectives Terry Pearson, Frank Nankivell, Jorge DelRio, and other officers also move toward Riverview and Kumler, while Sgt. Huber remains hidden in the alley observing the two cars.

39:41:29...
Hrs:Mins:Secs

"That car is moving. The Shadow's moving!"

Hiding in the Kumler house, the gang had noticed Sgt. Huber's police cruiser drive from their street a minute earlier and now worry they will be found out. They take the opportunity to bolt.

As soon as Taylor, Keene, Smith and Mathews jump in a car, Woodson hurriedly phones the police emergency operator a second time this day. Sandra Pinson speaks to the police as well.

39:42:08...
Hrs:Mins:Secs

Sgt. Perez presses the button and the high-pitched emergency "tone" is transmitted once again over the radio alerting responding officers of the potential danger they may encounter.

Perez: "Okay, crews...We just got the call at 7-2-9 Kumler. Got information that says a black Dodge Shadow parked in front. Supposed to be guns in the car. Subjects are stripping another stolen car at this time. Didn't say where.

"Three black male juveniles in the back yard; friends of the son. They were overhead, were overheard talking about how they had, uh, hit somebody and stolen their vehicle (slight pause).

PEREZ: "[Crew] 520, I'm gonna send somebody over there.... (pause) Okay, [Crew] 524A?"

CREW 524A: "Crew 524A, Riverview, and Belmonte Park."

PEREZ: "Okay, 4A, why don't you head over to 729 Kumler – 7-2-9 Kumler – and speak with Sandra [Pinson]. Give us any information you can on this."

CREW 524A: "Clear."

In what seemed to be mere moments after positioning himself in the alley, Sgt. Huber's heart jumps and he grabs his microphone.

HUBER: "[Crew] 520 [to] Dispatch. That car is moving! That Shadow's moving!"

The sergeant races to his police cruiser on Catalpa, places the car in gear and hits the gas, expecting the Shadow to be out of sight. Urgently, Sgt. Perez broadcasts a "Code A" allowing him to restrict the radio traffic to only Sgt. Huber.

Sgt. Huber's view of Kumler to his left, north across West Riverview

PEREZ: "Westside Channel, Code A! [Crew] 520, you've got it. We've got plenty of crews there. Just let 'em know what's going on."

Zipping to West Riverview Sgt. Huber turns right, is surprised to see the Shadow stopped at the intersection, and catches a glimpse of a man bolting from the car.

HUBER: "...North on Kumler! They're bailing out. They're still in the 700 block! ... They're still staying in it. White female; ah, black female; black male drivin'."

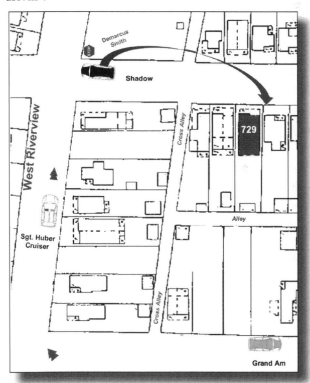

PEREZ: "Okay, use caution. They have guns."

HUBER: "Alright, I think a passenger got out and ran but I'm going to try to stop 'em. ... 1800 block of West Riverview."

As Demarcus Smith flees on foot toward the dead end of Kumler, Sgt. Huber slows while motioning to the driver to turn onto Riverview. Keene complies and heads toward Euclid Avenue. The sergeant pulls behind the Shadow, focusing on the three remaining suspects.

39:43:31...
Hrs:Mins:Secs

"*I wanted them to be Bonnie and Clyde.*"

Sgt. Huber hears a number of officers, including the Lawson brothers, advise they are close by so he activates his overhead lights to stop the vehicle.

 Police cars diagonally cut off the suspect car, while the Lawson brothers slam their vehicle to a halt in front of the black Dodge Shadow, blocking its forward movement ... boxing in the killers' car. Crews acknowledge their arrival.

CREW 524A: "I'm with ya."

CREW 961: "I'm with him."

Seeing the inrush of fellow officers, the sergeant hastily radios about the flight of the fourth suspect.

HUBER: "A subject in all black got out of the car when I started driving after it. He's gonna be down here at the dead end of Kumler somewhere."

Gun drawn, Sgt. Huber quickly approaches Keene urging he show his hands, totally unaware that Taylor is angrily demanding Keene shoot the sergeant ... shoot him now.

But in an instant, Det. Tom Lawson jumps on the hood of the car, pointing his Glock directly at the driver, ordering him not to move.

Swinging his pointed service weapon at the three killers, Sgt. Huber is quickly joined by other officers; they yell at the suspects to show their hands and to get out of the car. Surrounded, they're stunned by the rapid arrival of police.

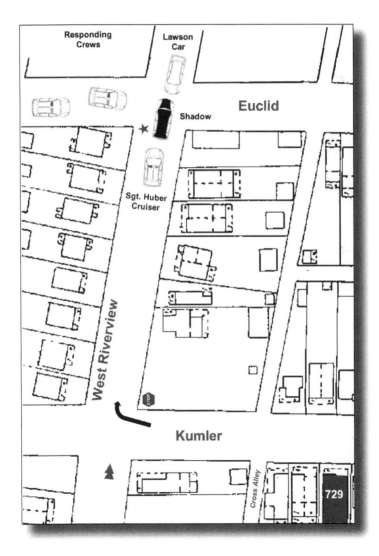

PEREZ: "Get the car stopped?"

CREW 522: "[The] car's stopped and they are [Signal] 20 (a radio broadcast code conveying all officers on the scene are 'safe')."

The three trapped suspects emerge from the vehicle, wearing the stolen jewelry and clothing of their murder victims.

STATE
& REGION

'They're just out for the blood'

Laura Taylor
(below)

Heather Mathews
(left) and
Marvalleous Keene

Now, the detectives and officers see the faces of cruelty this holiday weekend in Dayton.

Marvallous Keene is taken into custody by Det. Nankivell; Heather Mathews by Det. DelRio; and Laura Taylor by Sgt. Huber, who immediately turns her over to Det. Tom Lawson.

On the most frigid day of the week, this blood-lust gang of cold killers is apprehended without resistance.

DOYLE: "I wanted them to be Bonnie and Clyde, bad asses to the end and go out in a blaze of glory. They never do."

39:44:02...
HRS:MINS:SECS

The Fleeing Killer

As Detectives Tom and Wade Lawson arrange with the uniformed officers for the transport of the prisoners, two other detectives begin to search for the killer who had fled on foot.

CREW 983: "[Crew] 983. We need a better description of the passenger and which way he went?"

CREW 987: "Crew 987 [to] Radio (dispatch): Myself and [Crew] 986 are gonna be out on foot at the dead-end of Kumler for crews information."

PEREZ: "Okay, [Crew] 520 can you give us a better description of the other guy there … that ran?"

HUBER: "The driver of the car, the detectives are talking to him right now. I'm going back to the other stolen vehicle, the Grand Am, just in case he tries to get in it."

CREW 524A: "[Crew] 520, I'm down here with it now."

HUBER: "Okay. For the crews' information, maybe we'll just have the crew talk to Sandra [Pinson] and find out who the guy was in all black that got out of the car."

The murderer the crews are looking for is DeMarcus Smith, who, only moments before, had run inside the Kumler house. Passing Woodson at the doorway, Smith frantically yells back, "They got 'em! They got 'em!" before running upstairs to hide in a bedroom.

Woodson takes the cue to flee in the opposite direction … toward the cruiser lights and into the protective presence of police officers. Sgt. Huber spots him.

39:50:37…
HRS:MINS:SECS

HUBER: "Mr. Woodson's here on Kumler.... You're saying he was supposedly taken against his will, right?"

PEREZ: "That's what he says. Ah, I'd definitely separate him from everybody else. He's got some good information."

Sgt. Huber tries to determine if Woodson is a kidnap victim, witness, or suspect. Regardless, he will be taken to police headquarters and interviewed.

The captured killers are seated in police cars, and glare at Woodson as he anxiously talks to police. He knows it's all or nothing; if he thought he was a target before, he knows he is a dead man now. But the detective's work is not done.

Nick Woodson's Police mug shot

The priority is to capture the fourth killer. Detectives and officers canvass the neighborhood, talk amongst themselves, compare notes, and exchange radio transmissions.

It's now past two in the afternoon, over five minutes since the arrest of three murderers.

As he talks to Woodson, Sgt. Huber learns critical information which he relays to Det. Wade Lawson.

Police Dispatch clock displaying 1407 hours military - 2:07 p.m.

HUBER: "[Crew] 520 to 612."

W. LAWSON: "Go ahead... (pause) Go ahead 520."

HUBER: "Yeah, ah, in talking to the caller-in on this one (Woodson), are there weapons in the car? He said there should be."

Investigative Case File record of recovered weapons

```
                            WEAPONS

(1) .25 CAL. RAVEN ARMS MODEL MP-25 SEMI-AUTOMATIC PISTOL.
    (Chrome with white handle)

    Recovered: Under driver's seat of Dodge Shadow at time of
               arrest.

(2) .25 CAL. CZ MODEL DUO SEMI-AUTOMATIC PISTOL.
    (Black)

(3) .32 CAL. DAVIS INDUSTRIES MODEL D-32 DERRINGER PISTOL.

    Recovered: Rear passenger floor board of Dodge Shadow at time
               of arrest.
```

W. LAWSON: "Ah, yeah. There's a .25 [caliber gun] in the car."

39:55:10...
HRS:MINS:SECS

While the guns are being recovered from the car, Woodson identifies his aunt's house on Kumler to Sgt. Huber. The sergeant asks Det. Lawson to switch to a different radio channel for a private conversation.

W. LAWSON: "Go ahead [Crew]520."

HUBER: "Yeah, you guys may be way ahead of me on this one. Ah, I'm also receiving information they're responsible for 517 Neal. Do you have that too?"

W. LAWSON: "Sure do."

HUBER: "Okay. The guy I'm talking to seems ... doesn't know about a second black male getting out and running away but somebody was sitting in the front seat, I think."

W. LAWSON: "Okay, the person I talked to said two more people inside 729 Kumler ... part of the same group."

HUBER: "Okay. Apparently, the guy that got out went west between the houses on the south side of Riverview. I don't have a name on him yet. We will see what we can get."

W. LAWSON: "Okay, clear."

39:58:46...
HRS:MINS:SECS

Meanwhile, Detectives Terry Pearson and Frank Nankivell head to the house at 729 Kumler.

There they speak to the
Det. Pearson   resident, Nick Woodson's aunt Sandra Pinson, and guardedly enter the house.

Det. Nankivell

While asking if anyone else is home, the detectives look up to see a young black male descending the stairs.

The teen claims he is Deon Pinson, Woodson's cousin, but it soon becomes clear to the detectives that he is not who he says he is.

Police photo of
Demarcus Smith

Upon further questioning, the detectives conclude he is, in fact, Demarcus Smith.

They are looking into cold eyes of the fourth killer.

Police officers take him into custody and collect Smith's clothing, including Fila gym shoes belonging to Danita Gullette.

40 HOURS / **40:00:00.**
HRS:MINS:SECS

A mere 40 hours has passed since the four detectives were called out to Danita's murder scene.

Throughout this weekend, the Dayton investigators have been joined by coroner officials at recurring scenes of bloodshed to which they had been called. Now, the four detectives will tirelessly pursue the shooting cases and tie together these crimes.

The homicide squad is on the verge of bringing justice for the families of three Christmas murder victims: Danita, Richmond and Sarah.

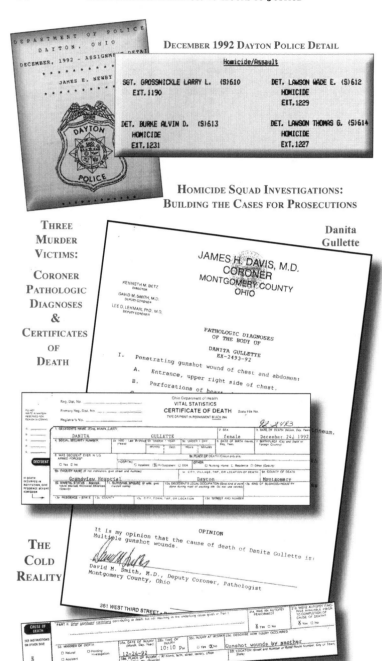

DECEMBER 1992 DAYTON POLICE DETAIL

Homicide/Assault

SGT. GROSSNICKLE LARRY L. (S)610	DET. LAWSON WADE E. (S)612
EXT.1190	HOMICIDE
	EXT.1229
DET. BURKE ALVIN D. (S)613	DET. LAWSON THOMAS G. (S)614
HOMICIDE	HOMICIDE
EXT.1231	EXT.1227

HOMICIDE SQUAD INVESTIGATIONS:
BUILDING THE CASES FOR PROSECUTIONS

THREE MURDER VICTIMS:

CORONER PATHOLOGIC DIAGNOSES & CERTIFICATES OF DEATH

THE COLD REALITY

Danita Gullette

JAMES H. DAVIS, M.D.
CORONER
MONTGOMERY COUNTY
OHIO

KENNETH M. BETZ
DIRECTOR

DAVID M. SMITH, M.D.
DEPUTY CORONER

LEE D. LEHMAN, PhD., M.D.
DEPUTY CORONER

PATHOLOGIC DIAGNOSES
OF THE BODY OF

DANITA GULLETTE
EX-2493-92

I. Penetrating gunshot wound of chest and abdomen:
  A. Entrance, upper right side of chest,
  B. Perforations of heart,

Ohio Department of Health
VITAL STATISTICS
CERTIFICATE OF DEATH State File No.
TYPE OR PRINT IN PERMANENT BLACK INK

DANITA GULLETTE female December 24, 1992

Grandview Hospital Dayton Montgomery

OPINION

It is my opinion that the cause of death of Danita Gullette is:
Multiple gunshot wounds.

David M. Smith, M.D., Deputy Coroner, Pathologist
Montgomery County, Ohio

361 WEST THIRD STREET

12-24-92 10:10 PM Gunshot wounds by another

Richmond
Maddox

Causes of
Deaths:

Gunshot
Wound

JAMES H. DAVIS, M.D.
CORONER
MONTGOMERY COUNTY
OHIO

Sarah
Abraham

CHAPTER 5

DAY AFTER CHRISTMAS
(Evening)

Miami Valley Regional Crime Laboratory
361 West Third Street   Dayton, Ohio 45402   513/225-4990   FAX 513/496-7916

Kenneth M. Betz, *Director*

January 4, 1993

TO: Det. W.E. Lawson
           Investigation Division

FROM: Mark T. Cordle/R.E. Swank, Jr.
           Latent Print Examiners

SUBJECT: Laboratory Case #92-12447 Joseph Wilkerson
           Homicide occurring at 3321 Prescott
           on December 27, 1992

Sir:

On December 27, 1992 the following exhibits were received
in the Identification Section for evaluation and
comparison against the listed subject:

Exhibit #1   Three latent print card(s) identified as
              being recovered from blue Pontiac Grand
              Am 2dr.

Exhibit #2   Known fingerprints (and/or) palmprints
              of 2a. Laura J. Taylor, 2b. Heather N.
              Mathews, 2c. Marvallous M. Keene, DPD
              #74038, and 2d. Demarcus M. Smith

The latent prints in Exhibit #1, developed by Officer J.
Burns/M.T. Cordle, were evaluated and found to be
suitable for identification purposes.

Upon comparison of Exhibit #1 (interior mirror) to
Exhibit #2b, it was determined that it is identical to
the right thumb of Heather N. Mathews. There are
sufficient points of comparison to make a positive
identification.

Upon comparison of Exhibit #1 (impressions from metal
between windshield and l. front door) to Exhibit #2c, it
was determined that it is identical to the right ring
finger of Marvallous M. Keene. There are sufficient
points of comparison to make a positive identification.

Dedicated to truth through forensic science

Crime Lab comparison of the suspects' fingerprints
to those recovered from the blue Pontiac Grand Am

1974 Buick Electra
Certificate of Title

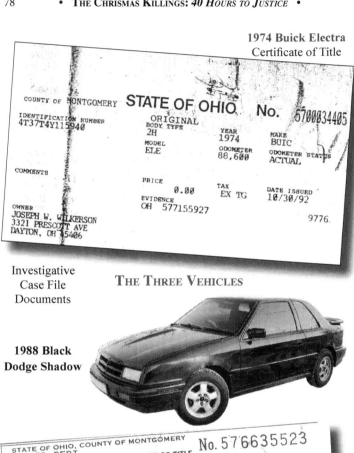

Investigative
Case File
Documents

THE THREE VEHICLES

**1988 Black
Dodge Shadow**

Certificate of Title
1989 Pontiac Grand Am

Piecing Together the Evidence

Even with Smith's arrest, the detectives are piecing together fragmented information gathered from the street and inside the house, only to discover that there are not just two cars used by the killers — the black Shadow stopped on Riverview and the blue Grand Am parked on Catalpa — but there is a third car involved: a red Buick Electra.

PEREZ: "[Crew] 612 and 520 hang on a second. [Crew] 612?"

W. LAWSON: "Go ahead."

PEREZ: "Yeah, on that information we got earlier … about … where they got the red car, did we ever get anything more that we can check where that's supposed to be?"

W. LAWSON: "I don't have that."

GROSSNICKLE: "[Crew] 610 to 612."

W. LAWSON: "Go ahead."

GROSSNICKLE: "If you got that gentleman we talked about before (Woodson), he says he can pretty much point that out."

Hearing the transmission, on-scene detectives ask Woodson about a red car. He reveals the gang used a red 1974 Buick Electra earlier in the day with plans to commit a hold-up in East Dayton. Officers run the registration of the Electra and learn the owner is Joseph Wilkerson of Prescott Avenue.

At the same time, a crew on Catalpa discovers the blue Grand Am is also registered to Wilkerson.

"They partied in his house for several days."
REVELATION FOR THE HOMICIDE SQUAD

Following up on the information, police arrive at Prescott

by 3 p.m. to speak to the owner of the two cars. No one answers, but the door is unlocked.

Upon entering, they find furniture in disarray, trash and items scattered throughout, and the kitchen in shambles.

A microwave and television appear to be missing ... the sign of a crime. Calling out to the owner, the officers receive no reply and head to the bedroom.

Dayton Daily News photo

Arms spread eagle and tied to the bed is the body of Joseph Wilkerson. His face and chest are covered with bloody bed clothes; his legs are protruding from a bloody blanket.

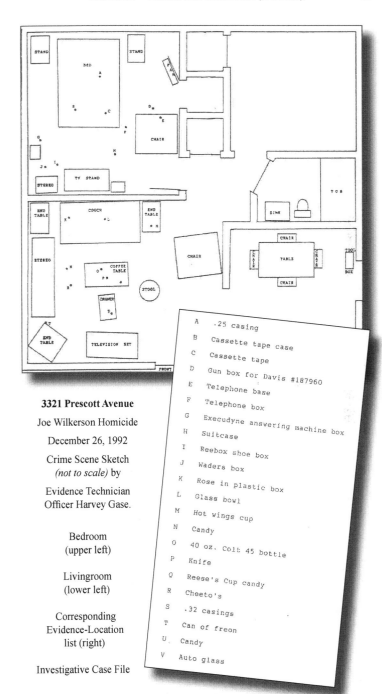

3321 Prescott Avenue

Joe Wilkerson Homicide

December 26, 1992

Crime Scene Sketch
(not to scale) by

Evidence Technician
Officer Harvey Gase.

Bedroom
(upper left)

Livingroom
(lower left)

Corresponding
Evidence-Location
list (right)

Investigative Case File

A   .25 casing

B   Cassette tape case

C   Cassette tape

D   Gun box for Davis #187960

E   Telephone base

F   Telephone box

G   Execudyne answering machine box

H   Suitcase

I   Reebox shoe box

J   Waders box

K   Rose in plastic box

L   Glass bowl

M   Hot wings cup

N   Candy

O   40 oz. Colt 45 bottle

P   Knife

Q   Reese's Cup candy

R   Cheeto's

S   .32 casings

T   Can of freon

U   Candy

V   Auto glass

Joe Wilkerson had been ruthlessly attacked. Police would soon learn that he was the gang's very first murder victim on Christmas Eve.

While ravaging his home, the group had displayed utter disregard for this man's security, dignity and life. Even more appalling to the officers is the realization that the gang members had returned to the home on Prescott several times after they killed Joe.

LARRY: "[They] partied in his house for several days, while he laid there in bed with clothes over top of him, dead."

Victim list from shooting rampage increases

(newspaper clipping, Dayton Daily News)

The discovery of this especially heinous crime is quickly relayed to the detectives at Police Headquarters interviewing the murder suspects.

The police officers on the scene report that Wilkerson's wrists are bound to the headboard with electrical cords. He has gunshot wounds to his head and chest.

An aluminum casing for a .25 caliber Blazer bullet is found in the bed, the same type of shell found beneath the pay phone and on the Mini Market floor.

Now the detectives have even more to discuss with the four murder suspects in custody.

"Hey, put some drama in your life."
Interrogations Part 1: Joseph Wilkerson Murder

At the Police Headquarters, Taylor, Keene, Smith, and Mathews have been separated for questioning. Sgt. Larry Grossnickle has been joined in the 'Dick Section' by Detectives Wade Lawson, Tom Lawson, and Doyle Burke.

Keene questioned by Wade Lawson

WADE: "...We took the four down to the police department... and we began the interviews. Marvallous just opened up and began talking....

"How it all started out, according to Marvallous, [was] they partied in Joe's house for two or three days and ate his food and just having

a great time and showing other people."

TOM: "They recruited Wendy and Marvin... 'Go with us.' One of the phrases that was used by Laura Taylor [was].... 'Hey put some drama in your life.'

"And that's when they took Wendy and Marvin to Joe's house and showed them, 'Hey, look what we did ... we killed this guy.'

"It's needless, it's senseless ... but that's how these people were."

"Merry Christmas, bitch."
INTERROGATIONS PART 2: DANITA GULLETTE MURDER

The interrogations continue. The detectives elicit greater detail from three of the four murder suspects.

WADE: "And the three except Laura Taylor gave what we thought were complete confessions."

What the detectives learn is that the group fancied themselves a gang. They had been downtown looking for a quick score but failed when trying to rob a trick. Looking for another victim to rob, the group traveled on Neal Avenue and came upon Danita Gullette at a pay phone.

WADE: "Gullette on the phone ... they walked up and said, 'Merry Christmas, bitch,' and began shooting her.... 'Merry Christmas, bitch' and boom, boom, boom, boom ... shot nine times."

Pointing his finger as if holding a gun, Doyle reimagines the moment of the crime and its senseless nature.

Doyle: "Danita was trapped in that phone booth.... How to just go up to somebody [and say], 'Merry Christmas bitch, here you go,' [then] walk out with a pair of gym shoes [and] take somebody's five-to-six-dollars-worth of items?"

"BOOM! She just pulls out a gun and shoots him."
Interrogations Part 3: Richmond Maddox Murder

During the suspects' interviews, the detectives also find that former boyfriends were convenient victims.

They learn that Smith had shot Jeffrey Wright, Mathews' ex-boyfriend, four times on Christmas Eve though Wright survived the attempted murder.

The detectives further learn that Taylor began targeting her old boyfriend Richmond Maddox hours later and – in a botched robbery attempt – executed him with one shot to the temple.

Tom: "...From the interviews we did with the three that talked, they talked and bragged among themselves about what they had done...

TOM: "And Laura Taylor bragged [to friends] about how she shot Richmond Maddox... He's driving down the street makes a turn and there's a car following him... He tells her, 'I think that car is following me.'

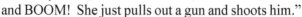

"That's why he turns on Benton, a little bitty street, a one block street, and BOOM! She just pulls out a gun and shoots him."

During the interrogation, even the most seasoned of the four homicide investigators, Det. Wade Lawson, is taken aback by Taylor's insolence in the face of serious charges.

Taylor's demure and slight appearance belied her cold-heartedness.

WADE: "I don't think I've ever met, what I would call, a hardened person at 16 years old. A cold-hearted girl.

"She was so hard, she didn't even go to the restroom or ask to go to the restroom, she urinated in the [interview room] chair she was sitting in.... Hope I never run into another person like her.

VICTIM	.25 RAVEN	.25 CZ DUO	.32 DERRINGER
Gulette	(Keene?)	(Smith?)	------
Wright	(Smith)	------	------
Maddox	------	------	(Taylor)
Abraham/Pettus	(Keene)	(Smith)	(?)

Investigative Case File record tying the
murder weapons to the killers

"It just never ended."

Interrogations Part 4: Sarah Abraham Murder

As the interviews progress, the detectives learn about the gang's efforts to victimize others in the Dayton community...

... in an attempted robbery in Yuma Court; ... at an ATM on Germantown Street; ... traveling to the east side of Dayton looking for victims to rob; ... twice at an ATM on Salem Avenue; and ... the aggravated robbery in the county at a BP station on Salem.

And, now, the detectives delve into their callout of that very morning – the robbery and multiple shootings at the Short Stop Mini Market.

Wade: "I think a lot about Sarah Abraham at the store.

"Very lovely lady, 11-year-old daughter... she did exactly what they said. 'Give me the money,' she gave them the money. Had the gun right in her face, and why kill her?

"I mean you've got the money, you can walk out.

"But I think they just took pleasure in pulling the trigger and seeing her die. I don't understand that. I cannot understand that. I don't want to understand that."

Tom: "It's like a serial killer but more than that it was a spree killing ... none of them made sense."

Solid evidence from the firearms used by the killers bind the crimes.

Investigative Case File record of recovered ammunition

AMMUNITION

Dodge Shadow: 44 live .25 cal. Blazer

729 Kumler: 11 live rounds .25 cal Blazer

Laura Taylor: 8 live .32 cartridges

Marvallous Keene: 2 live .32 cartridges
                    at time of arrest.

DOYLE: "It was an aluminum case disposable ammunition; it was not popular at that time. And to have that at one scene was kind of an anomaly, no big deal. But starting to have it at other scenes, that's what really tied it together, initially....

"We had both guns that tied in the .32 caliber ... and everything's coming together."

The detectives' interviews uncover numerous felonious and capital offenses – three stolen vehicles, armed robberies, calculated murders. And the crimes paint a horrendous picture. Three of the four killers confess.

No fewer than 10 innocent people shot or threatened with death; three lie wounded in area hospitals and three are dead with one more to die within days. All of the pieces of the puzzle have seemingly been assembled..."

DOYLE: "... but it just never ended."

The Great Miami River looking north toward the Courts Building

Night falls in Dayton while police evidence crews continue work on Prescott Avenue.

Detective Wade Lawson's investigation "To-Do" list

CHAPTER 6
CHRISTMAS SUNDAY

A Dayton View church steeple appears in the dawn.

Cleveland Plain Dealer Article

Downtown Dayton

Newspaper headlines

Revelation and Recovery

After a week of gloom, clouds, and frigid air – attended by public fear – the citizens of Dayton awake to the revelation that the senseless acts of random violence this holiday of 1992 are, in fact, connected.

Before the murders were discovered to be linked, the press had reported them a day at a time. The details of a young woman's Christmas Eve murder was startling when reported the following day in Friday's news.

The Saturday press account of a second killing in another respectable Dayton neighborhood on Christmas evening was alarming.

But, on Sunday morning, when the newspapers described the market shootings from the day before as well as the discovery of a body on Prescott Avenue, the community was horrorstruck.

The press would coin the slaughter:

"The Christmas Killings"

DENNIS: "I remember reading in the Sunday newspaper about a dark story … that the Dayton police had successfully linked a weekend series of local slayings and made arrests."

Police link slayings

"I also have this vivid recollection of Christmas Sunday opening with clear skies, morning sunshine and the temperature growing into the 40s once again. My wife had given birth to our baby on Christmas Eve, and the world seemed like it was bright."

In fact, puffs of white clouds brush a lovely blue sky. The warming air and the delicate chirrup of birds enliven Christmas Sunday. Morning church bells ring throughout Dayton; people congregate to rejoice.

Feeling positive about their investigation, believing that a deadly menace has ended, the four Dayton detectives are able to enjoy a good night's sleep unlike the killers in the custody of police.

Life in Dayton reclaims a sense of normalcy.

Christmas Sunday is a day of spiritual celebration for the community.

"Laura Taylor told me!"

Religious services are being held throughout the Dayton area. At a Westside church, the Reverend William Head, who also serves as chief investigator of the Dayton branch of the NAACP, is troubled by the news of a petite 16-year old held in custody at a juvenile detention center for her involvement in a terrible spree of murders that occurred over the Christian holiday.

The minister takes it upon himself to visit Taylor on this Sunday for a pastoral counseling session, then hears from her a shocking revelation.

DOYLE: "Reverend Head called and said, 'I can tell you where two more bodies are that Laura Taylor told me.'"

The ringing church bells have silenced. Chill assails the air as clouds of gray once again sweep in with the dark of winter.

It's 4:45 p.m.

"I mean, these were friends."
Discovery by the Homicide Squad

As a blanket of winter darkness cloaks Dayton, the detectives follow through on the tip from the local minister.

The detectives make a gruesome discovery at the gravel pit visited by the gang the day before. Behind a mound, Marvin Washington had been massacred ... shot 10 times ... Wendy Cottrill savagely shot three times, her gym shoes wrenched from her feet. This couple was the last to die.

Pathways in the gravel yard where the murder victims are recovered

Police: Group had hit list

Gravel pit crime scene sketch from the Investigative Case File
submitted by evidence technician, Off. Marshall Manning

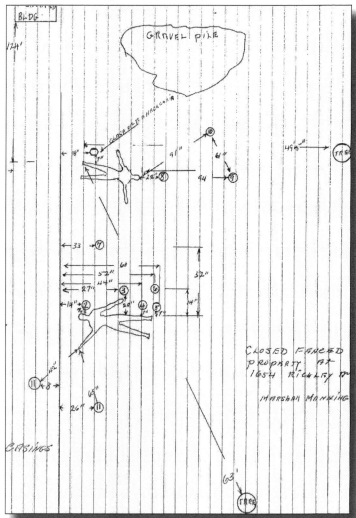

Dayton Daily News

EDITORIAL

For the killers, all lines seem to have been erased from the psyche.

The question is "Why? How could they do it?"

LARRY: "They turned around and killed one of their buddies because they didn't want to be caught. I mean, I don't know that I've been on a homicide investigation that's been any more ruthless."

TOM: "Six people are dead, two more shot ... other potential, had they been at the wrong place ... would have been dead. Just these senseless actions of these four people."

Nick Woodson's gripping intuition had been revealed by the fate of his friends.

WADE: "Woodson knew what was about to happen... He knows they are going to kill. He says, 'Drop me  off at my house....' They took Wendy and Washington out to the gravel pit... and I mean these were friends. Four kids get out of the car and Wendy was like 16 years old and they stuck a gun in her mouth and pulled the trigger." I worked homicide a long time and you can't figure it out. I can't."

Did cravings for drugs and money fuel the gang's actions? Were the Posse's cold-blooded murders of innocents driven by wolf-pack euphoria? Or were the killings motivated by acts of dominance that mutated into fearful self-preservation?

Even to veteran detectives, the motive for the senseless acts by this gang remains a mystery decades later. In 1992, a Dayton Daily News editorial asked, "How could they do it?" The question is unanswered. All that detectives and the community can do is to reflect on the vicious nature of the acts.

EPILOGUE

"THE CHRISTMAS KILLINGS"

Jail cell block on the Dayton Safety Building 4th floor.

–Photograph courtesy of retired Det. Michelle Moser

Sgt. Larry Grossnickle – Det. Wade Lawson – – Det. Tom Lawson – Det. Doyle Burke

REFLECTING

Sobering experiences recounted inside *The Embassy*

THE STORY

One 18-year-old mother was killed, apparently for her shoes.
One had a car.
One was a store clerk who had $30 in the cash register.
One had no money.
Two knew too much.
The three-day shooting rampage that left six people dead and two wounded during Christmas was unlike any in Dayton's history.
Joseph Wilkerson, Danita Gullette, Richmond Maddox, Sara Abraham, Marvin Washington and Wendy Cottrill died during those three days for reasons that make little sense.
Following the murders, the events of those three days have trickled out.

Heather Mathews   DeMarcus Smith   Laura Taylor   Marvallous Keene

Reflections: The Viciousness of the Crimes

DENNIS: "During the week after Christmas, the details of the 'Christmas Killings' were daily news. It was incredible to read and it made me worry about the safety of my wife and newborn child."

"It was especially shocking because one of the murders suspects, Heather Mathews, had been a classmate of mine at Belmont High School. She was a non-descript person and to learn she was capable of participating in these kinds of crimes was something I just couldn't fathom."

DOYLE: "No one was safe, they would kill anybody, just look at them cross-eyed."

LARRY: "They shot and killed everybody that was defenseless [who] didn't even realize it was coming."

TOM: "Joe Wilkerson, ... laying there in bed. Laura, after he's shot in the chest [by Keene], said, 'Let me show you how to do this,' and point blank shoots him in the head and brags to the others 'this is how you do this.' "

"And then taking Wendy and Marvin into the house and showing them Joe, him laying there dead in bed and what they had done, and they were proud of it. And they were having fun doing it."

WADE: "Laura Taylor was about as hard as that. And I always said that she was the leader. I mean I think that she controlled Marvallous but he had to be willing."

DOYLE: "She was one that was clearly the brains of the operation and he was the front man. She would say go and he would do it."

WADE: "How it all started out, according to Marvallous, he and Laura Taylor in the motel room downtown Dayton and they were out of money and she said:

'I know a guy who works at GM. He's always got money. We will go to his house and we'll go in and he'll think we are there for sex and we'll rob him and kill him.'

"And they walked over to Yuma Place and crossed into lower Dayton View and walked three miles to Joe's house....

"He let them in, of course, and they got him back to the bedroom and tied him up.... Marvallous, I believe, fired the first shot, shot him in the stomach and then Laura shot him in the head.

"But the part that even to this day is hard to believe is they went out ... and told Nick about what they had done and a couple other people."

And the gang continued its shooting spree...Danita Gullette, Jeffrey Wright, Richmond Maddox, Jones Pettus, Sarah Abraham. And the rampage was no secret among their friends.

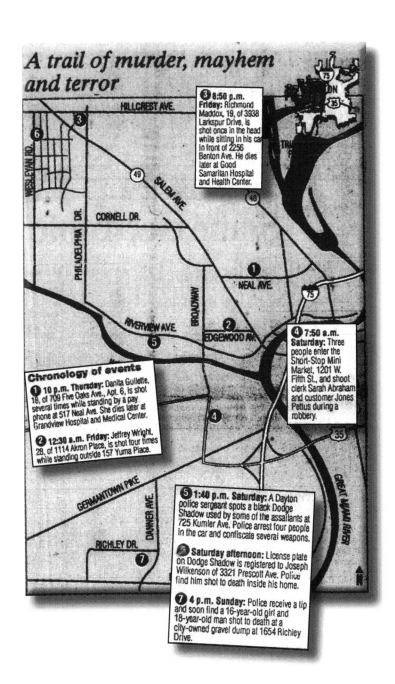

A trail of murder, mayhem and terror

❸ 6:50 p.m. Friday: Richmond Maddox, 19, of 3938 Larkspur Drive, is shot once in the head while sitting in his car in front of 2256 Benton Ave. He dies later at Good Samaritan Hospital and Health Center.

❹ 7:50 a.m. Saturday: Three people enter the Short-Stop Mini Market, 1201 W. Fifth St., and shoot clerk Sarah Abraham and customer Jones Pettus during a robbery.

Chronology of events

❶ 10 p.m. Thursday: Danita Gullette, 16, of 709 Five Oaks Ave., Apt. 6, is shot several times while standing by a pay phone at 517 Neal Ave. She dies later at Grandview Hospital and Medical Center.

❷ 12:30 a.m. Friday: Jeffrey Wright, 28, of 1114 Akron Place, is shot four times while standing outside 157 Yuma Place.

❺ 1:40 p.m. Saturday: A Dayton police sergeant spots a black Dodge Shadow used by some of the assailants at 725 Kumler Ave. Police arrest four people in the car and confiscate several weapons.

❻ Saturday afternoon: License plate on Dodge Shadow is registered to Joseph Wilkenson of 3321 Prescott Ave. Police find him shot to death inside his home.

❼ 4 p.m. Sunday: Police receive a tip and soon find a 16-year-old girl and 18-year-old man shot to death at a city-owned gravel dump at 1654 Richley Drive.

HILLCREST AVE.

WESLEYAN RD.

PHILADELPHIA DR.

CORNELL DR.

SALEM AVE.

NEAL AVE.

BROADWAY

RIVERVIEW AVE.

EDGEWOOD AVE.

GERMANTOWN PIKE

DANNER AVE.

RICHLEY DR.

GREAT MIAMI RIVER

LARRY: "Nick Woodson was the only smart one of the bunch because he saw the line being dwindled toward him and he was about to get it. I don't make Nick

Woodson to be a big hero. He was smart, but he knew his time was up and it damn near was."

WADE: "And that's where Wendy and Washington got in trouble because they knew about that.... I don't understand ... but that's just a little more ... of how they think. No remorse. I never saw any remorse...."

Exterior (above)

Prisoner passageway between the Dayton Safety Building and the Montgomery County Jail

Interior (right)

Prosecution and Sentencing

The spotlight on these murders spreads far outside the Dayton area. The spree of Christmas killings is so horrifying that it captures the attention of the national and international press. It is a worldwide news story in the print media and early days of cable news.

The prosecution of the Christmas killers is the responsibility of the Montgomery County Prosecutor, Mathias Heck, Jr. He assigns James Levinson and Angela Frydman to pursue charges. Lisa Edwards, the Montgomery County Victim-Witness Advocate, cares for the families of the murder victims throughout the course of the trials.

Bonds set at $5 million in killing spree

DAYTON (AP) — A judge set $5 million cash bonds yesterday

Judge Dan Gehres sets bail at the arraignment for the adult murder suspects, Keene and Mathews, at five million dollars each.

Then, in the spring of 1993, the juvenile court rules that 16-year-old Laura Taylor and 17-year-old Demarcus Smith should be tried as adults and thus face a maximum penalty of life imprisonment.

DOYLE: "We mine for diamonds.... We photograph everything, take all the evidence we can and hope that one day we'll get to get a dividend out of it....

"It's just the best feeling when you do get it all together, you go, 'Man I'm glad we did that. I'm glad we got all this and now it's all coming together....' It just comes from experience. You just continue doing it."

TOM: "We do what we do, we gather the evidence and we have that evidence ready to be presented in a courtroom....

"In the courtroom it's presented and these people are found guilty and, at the end of the day, we are successful in what we've done."

Heather Mathews is indicted on two capital murder charges but accepts a plea bargain agreement in August 1993 in exchange for her testimony as a lead prosecution witness against Keene, Taylor, and Smith.

Marvallous Keene stands trial in September 1993 in Montgomery County Common Pleas Court. In January 1994, Laura Taylor is tried in Montgomery County Common Pleas Court. A month later, Smith opts out of a trial and pleads guilty to over a dozen felonious offenses.

Convicted of their many gross acts of violence, prison sentences are subsequently handed down and the killers never again pose a threat to the innocent in the Dayton community.

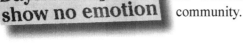

Dayton suspects show no emotion

HEATHER MATHEWS – Convicted of two counts of Aggravated Murder, two counts of Attempted Aggravated Murder, Conspiracy to Commit Aggravated Murder, five counts of Aggravated Robbery, as well as Burglary and Receiving Stolen Property.

Mathews is sentenced to 182 years in prison. Currently incarcerated in the Ohio Reformatory for Women, Mathews is eligible for parole in 2132.

DEMARCUS SMITH – Convicted of four counts of Aggravated Murder, two counts of Attempted Aggravated Murder, two counts of Kidnapping, five counts of Aggravated Robbery, as well as Felonious Assault and Burglary.

Smith is sentenced to 186 years in prison. Currently incarcerated in Mansfield Correctional Institute, Smith is ineligible for parole until 2125.

LAURA TAYLOR – Convicted of two counts of Aggravated Murder and one of Murder, two counts of Attempted Aggravated Murder, four counts of Aggravated Robbery, as well as Burglary.

This youngest, most diminutive and, arguably, the driving force of the murder spree is sentenced to the least time – 133 years in prison. Currently incarcerated in the Ohio Reformatory for Women, Taylor is ineligible for parole until 2097.

MARVALLOUS KEENE – The self-proclaimed leader of the "Downtown Posse" is convicted of five counts of Aggravated Murder, two counts of Attempted Aggravated Murder, two counts of Kidnapping, six counts of Aggravated Robbery,

as well as Aggravated Burglary and Burglary.

Keene is sentenced to serve consecutive terms in the penitentiary for a collective 133 to 305 years ending at Lucasville Prison.

Although the maximum punishment for Keene projects to the year 2298, only a window of time would be relevant because this killer is justifiably condemned to five death sentences.

The years pass slowly by: 1993 – 1994 – 1995 – 1996 – 1997 – 1998 – 1999 – 2000 – 2001 – 2002 – 2003 – 2004 – 2005 – 2006 – 2007 – 2008 – 2009 … *July 21, 2009*.

Clemency in the case of Marvallous Keene was initiated by the Ohio Parole Board, but the killer declines the opportunity to be interviewed. On death row in Lucasville Prison at 9:43 a.m., intravenous lines containing a lethal mix of three drugs flow into his veins. A mass killer is legally executed by the State of Ohio.

Time will pass even more slowly for three remaining Christmas killers. Removed from civilized society, these reprehensible convicts will all die caged long before 2097, 2125 and 2132.

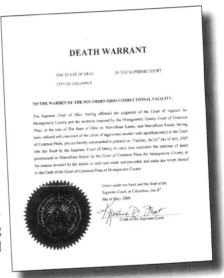

As for the homicide detectives, their quests for justice continue.

While attention to the greatest detail is key to their work, their dedication to duty is not solely rooted in police science and evidence gathering. Detectives pursue leads on behalf of the victims to avenge the mortal sins that cut short their lives … to resolve for their families the truth at the core of their terrible loss … to deliver a sense of justice and closure.

Justice and Closure

DETECTIVE WADE E. LAWSON
26½-Year Dayton Police Career
8-19-1969 to 1-3-1996

Post-Police Career
Montgomery County, Ohio
Coroner's Investigator

2012 EMBASSY INTERVIEW:

"Now the years I worked homicide we had four to five groups ... but none were more vicious than the Christmas killers. They're right at the top of the list. I don't know how you can get any worse."

Photo circa 1992

DETECTIVE THOMAS G. LAWSON
27-Year Dayton Police Career
2-3-1969 to 1-3-1996

Post-Police Career
Montgomery County, Ohio
Coroner's Investigator

2012 EMBASSY INTERVIEW:

"After 20 years we're still talking about this. And it's still fresh in my memory, I didn't read reports or anything before doing this interview, and it's still fresh in my mind after 20 years."

Photo circa 1992

SERGEANT MOISES PEREZ
33-Year Dayton Police Career
1-4-1982 to 4-24-2015

Post-Police Career
Grandview Medical Center
Investigative Sergeant

1992 DISPATCH TRANSMISSION:

"Attention all crews. All crews, be on the lookout for possible homicide suspects. Looking for a four-door black Shadow. It's definitely gonna be worth stopping them."

Photo circa 2012

LIEUTENANT JOHN H. HUBER
34-Year Dayton Police Career
1-18-1977 to 1-14-2011

Post-Police Career
Sinclair Community College
Chief of Public Safety

1992 DISPATCH TRANSMISSION:

"Crew 520 to Dispatch. That car is moving! That Shadow's moving! North on Kumler! They're bailing out.... but I'm going to try to stop 'em. .... 1800 block of West Riverview."

Photo circa 2012

DETECTIVE A. DOYLE BURKE
28-Year Dayton Police Career
2-1-1979 to 3-5-2007

Post-Police Career
Warren County, Ohio
Coroner's Investigator

Photo circa 1992

2012 EMBASSY INTERVIEW:

"Hats off to our uniformed guys ... We work with them and they work with us, everybody. All we had to say is 'it's a black car and it has four wheels' and they [will] work night and day trying to find that for us. I mean you can't beat that."

SERGEANT LARRY L. GROSSNICKLE
26½-Year Dayton Police Career
12-22-1969 to 7-26-1996

Post-Police Career
Fully Retired

Photo circa 1992

2012 EMBASSY INTERVIEW:

"It's always worked because we are a team, but that team also is the neighborhood, it's the people out there.... you are only as good as the relationships that you build within the community. And if you can't build those within the community then you are never going to be able to solve these things....

And that is what makes it work, that partnership."

In Memoriam

The Montgomery County Prosecutor's Office
Victim/Witness Mission Statement *(in excerpt)*

"There is sacredness in tears.
They are not the mark of weakness but of power....
They are messengers ... of unspeakable love."
—Washington Irving

Joseph Wilkerson
Age 34
7-3-1958 to 12-24-1992

Danita Gullette
Age 18
7-6-1974 to 12-24-1992

Richmond Maddox
Age 19
12-27-1972 to 12-25-1992

Wendy Cottrill
Age 16
6-13-1976 to 12-26-1992

Marvin Washington
Age 18
1-14-1974 to 12-26-1992

Sarah Abraham
Age 38
12-12-1954 to 12-31-1992

We Remember Them...

"In the blowing of the wind and in the chill of winter, we remember them.... In the beginning of the year and when it ends, we remember them .... So long as we live, they too shall live for they are now a part of us as we remember them."

—In excerpt from Gates of Prayer

Afterword

A Dedicated Team of Homicide Detectives

When I first became involved in this project, I knew very little about the world of law enforcement, as I had had few interactions with police during my lifetime. However, as I learned more about the demands placed on police officers in general and homicide detectives in particular, I began to develop a new respect for the service they commit to and the sacrifices they make.

Homicide detectives put in long, irregular hours. But it's not just a time commitment. Rather, it's the kind of work required of them – that they pay attention to every detail in a crime scene; that they compartmentalize the gruesome nature of what they see; that they demonstrate empathy toward victims' families; that they articulately testify in court the minute details of a crime – and the physical, mental, and emotional toll it all can take on them.

The senseless killings of six people during the 1992 Christmas season in Dayton, Ohio were heartbreaking, and nothing will ever alleviate the pain or lessen the loss experienced by the victims' families and friends.

The only salve for these emotional wounds might be knowing that the persistence and precision demonstrated by the homicide detectives in this narrative – **Wade Lawson, Tom Lawson, Larry Grossnickle**, and **Doyle Burke** – were the driving force behind successfully solving this tragic murder spree, tying together evidence from the killings for prosecutors.

Unravelling the complexity of these crimes within a span of 40 hours required excellent investigative skills and unending patience, while working under pressure to solve the crimes as quickly as possible to prevent more carnage.

The detectives' diligence, persistence, and dedication, as well as collaboration with their observant fellow uniformed officers – **John Huber**, **Moises Perez** and others – allowed the perpetrators to be apprehended and brought to justice.

Though these detectives' careers in law enforcement spanned several decades, it is perhaps their work in the case of the Christmas Killings that may be most significant.

For their dedication to their mission and their commitment to public service, we thank them.

—Judith Monseur

PHOTOGRAPHS – IMAGES

Austin Kirkpatrick is the graphic designer of the book cover. Several of the featured photographs appearing in this book are courtesy of **Elizabeth Weeks** (Chapter 1), **Carolyn J. Burns** (Chapter 3), retired Dayton Police Detective **Michelle Moser** (Epilogue), and retired Dayton Police Sergeant **Roger Edwards** (Chapter 3). He also provided photographs of all of the Dayton police buildings that appear in the book.

Nearly all of the courtroom and crime scenes are snapshots images from 1992 television file footage graciously provided by **Megan O'Rourke** who was a WDTN newscaster in 2012.

Virtually all of the images of newspaper articles from 1992 Christmas week and week after were provided either by **Bill Stolz**, archivist for Wright State University's Special Collections and Archives or from the personal collection of the Honorable Judge **Daniel Gehres**.

As mentioned in "Acknowledgements" (page v), **John Huber** and **Moises Perez** provided personal pictures of themselves in uniform. They were prompt in fulfilling requests made of them at the deadline for publication.

Dennis Murphy took photographs of Dayton street scenes to match the storyline, a dozen of which appear in the book, and all photographs of the four detectives inside the Embassy were taken in 2012 on behalf of DPH Foundation by former Dayton Police Officer **Amy Simpson**.

All other photographs and images shown without attribution are from these sources: The Dayton Metro Library, Montgomery Historical Society (now Dayton History), City of Dayton, Dayton Police Department, online public domain, as well as the private collection of Dayton Police History Foundation, Inc.

All proceeds from the sale of this book go to
Dayton Police History Foundation, Inc.
to further its educational goals.

Donations to support the efforts of DPH Foundation, Inc.
are gratefully accepted and receipted. Please mail to:

DPH FOUNDATION, INC.
P.O. BOX 293157
DAYTON, OHIO 45429-9157

or visit

DAYTONPOLICEHISTORY.ORG

DAYTON POLICE HISTORY FOUNDATION, INC.

Dayton Police History Foundation, Inc. is an outgrowth of a 2008 six-month police exhibit at Carillon Historical Park, *Patrolling the Streets of Dayton.* It was the largest temporary exhibit held at the park's newest museum facility at that time, the Dicke Family Transportation Center. It was visited by 20,000 students and, by that measure alone, was a success.

Dayton Police History Foundation, Inc. was officially chartered by the State of Ohio on January 1, 2010. It is a private, non-profit, 501(c)(3) charitable organization strictly dedicated to the preservation of local police history.

DPH Foundation, Inc. is an independent organization operating in cooperation with the city of Dayton Police Department, the Dayton Fraternal Order of Police, the Dayton History-NCR Archive Center, Carillon Historical Park and many other organizations. More can be learned about DPH Foundation at the following website:

DAYTONPOLICEHISTORY.ORG

CONTACT OR COMMENT:
INFO@DAYTONPOLICEHISTORY.ORG

2017 DPH BOARD OF TRUSTEES
John A. 'Jack' Barstow, Chairman
Stephen C. Grismer
William A. 'Alex' Heckman
Timothy D. Kennaley
James G. 'Jimmy' Mullins
Dennis A. Murphy
Mary L. Oliver

ABOUT THE AUTHORS

D ET. DENNIS MURPHY is a 17-year veteran of the Dayton Police Department. He entered the police academy in 2000 and worked both patrol in the 5th District and investigative assignments. In 2005, he was assigned to the Narcotics Bureau where he worked drug enforcement, vice and dignitary protection details. In 2009, Dennis was reassigned to the Homicide Squad and remained in that position through 2016 and throughout the writing of this book. Dennis is presently assigned to the Professional Standards Bureau as an Internal Affairs investigator.

 Dennis is one of the three founding members of Dayton Police History Foundation, Inc. and has the distinction of serving as its first chairman. He is one of the two active-duty Dayton police officers on the DPHF Board of Trustees. Dennis' interest in history is rooted in his Irish heritage and East Dayton upbringing. Dennis was an illustrator for "Patrolling the Streets of Dayton," the 2008 Dayton Police History Exhibit at Carillon Historical Park. He is a freelance artist specializing in comic illustration as a penciller and is currently contributing to an upcoming crime book by another author.

D R. JUDITH MONSEUR is a long-time educator whose career expands across higher education institutions, public schools, and state government, where she has led educational reform initiatives, managed federal and state grants, and taught pre-service and career teachers and principals. Her professional research includes the history of education, the socio-political context of education, and the expansion of equitable educational opportunities for underserved students.

From its very inception, the mission of the Dayton Police History Foundation and this project appealed to her interest in exploring the importance of civil service to a highly functioning democratic society.

A native Daytonian, Judith serves as Assistant Director at the Systems Development & Improvement Center at the University of Cincinnati. She holds a Ph.D. in Educational Policy and Leadership from The Ohio State University, a Masters of Humanities from Wright State University, and a B.S. in Education from The Ohio State University.

S GT. STEPHEN GRISMER (RET.) is a 25-year veteran of the Dayton Police Department. He entered the police academy in 1976 and was assigned to uniform patrol duties in the Fifth District. Promoted in 1986, he experienced a broad career in investigations, staff, internal affairs, drug enforcement, intelligence and training. He was a member of the hostage negotiation team and the vice president of the Dayton Fraternal Order of Police. He is a 1984 graduate of the University of Dayton with a degree concentration in journalism and a minor in criminal justice.

In 2008 he helped produce the successful police exhibit at Carillon Historical Park, *Patrolling the Streets of Dayton.* Currently, he is a member of the Dayton Police History Foundation, Inc. Board of Trustees. In 2013, Steve authored the book, *Drenched Uniforms and Battered Badges – How Dayton Police Emerged from the 1913 Flood,* to commemorate the 100th anniversary of one of the worst natural disasters in U.S history and pay tribute to the role of law enforcement in the rescue and relief efforts.

22183224R00081

Made in the USA
Lexington, KY
13 December 2018